THE BLUEPRINT
to EXCELLENCE
BEING, GROWING, LEADING, SOARING

16 SUCCESS PRINCIPLES
THAT LEAD TO EXCELLENCE

**Based on the famous teachings of
Booker T. Washington and Character Leadership**

━━━━━◦━━━━━

**A Personal & Professional Development Guide
Written by the Great-granddaughter of Booker T. Washington,
Dr. Sarah Washington O'Neal Rush**

 **Keshri
Publishing**

Dedication

This work is dedicated to my great-grandfather, whose shoulders I stand on—former slave, turned famous educator, and founder of Tuskegee University—Booker T. Washington. Thank you for your drive, determination, desire, and courage to rise above the unimaginable conditions of slavery. Thank you for laying a strong foundation and leaving an incredible legacy for us to build upon. Because of what you did, I can lead others who aspire to grow to new heights despite every obstacle.

SPECIAL NOTES

The **brick** images at the top of the page in the beginning of each quadrant and the quadrant *Wrap Up* sections were created by the author, Dr. Sarah Rush. She used a photo of one of the original bricks that Booker T. Washington and his students and faculty—former slaves and their descendants, used to build the original buildings on the campus of Tuskegee Institute, now known as Tuskegee University. She acquired the brick from one of the original buildings which was being demolished at the time of one of her visits to the school.

The ***Lifting the Veil Statue*** images beneath the title of each principle, are of the historical monument on the campus of Tuskegee University. Dedicated in 1922, the Booker T. Washington National Monument stands at the center of Tuskegee University's campus. Individuals and groups from all over the world come to take photos in front of this famous statue. The statue represents Booker T. Washington lifting a veil from the face of a former slave and pointing him to progress through education and industry.

Final Note: Unless otherwise noted, the quotations throughout this workbook are from Booker T. Washington.

TABLE OF CONTENTS

Sixteen-Success Principles Creed

16

16 Principles that cultivate attitudes of *Being, Growing, Leading,* and *Soaring*

Building Healthy Self-Worth ~ Being
"The individual who puts the most into life is the individual who gets the most out of life."

- **Mind**—Choose to awaken and improve daily
- **Body**—Embrace and Guard that which enfolds your heart, mind, and soul
- **Character**—Build a foundation grounded in sound values and principles
- **Confidence**—Allow no one to rob you of it

Managing through Change ~ Growing
"It is only through the surmounting of difficulties that individuals are made powerful."

- **Trials and Resilience**—Employ as lessons en route to success
- **Responsibility**—Discover personal power through action
- **Relationships**—Invest mental and emotional energy wisely
- **Faith**—Embrace hope and peace beyond understanding

Leading by Example ~ Leading
"One cannot hold another down in a ditch without staying down in the ditch with him."

- **Vision**—Advance your reach by expanding your vision
- **Education**—Always Seek endless opportunities to learn something new
- **Dignity of Work**—Keep in mind, we reap what we sow
- **Financial Responsibility**—Develop intelligent habits of spending, saving, and giving

Excelling in Perseverance ~ Soaring
"No man discouraged ever wins a victory."

- **Gratitude**— Determine to find moments to be grateful for daily
- **Purpose**—Establish through life experience, surroundings, and passion
- **Service**—Engage in making the world better than you found it
- **Excellence**—Strive to achieve with practice, discipline, & conscious choices.

ABOUT BOOKER T WASHINGTON

"The years come but once, and swiftly pass on, bearing the ineffaceable record we place upon them. If we make them beautiful years, we must do it moment by moment as they glide before us."
~Booker T. Washington

THE INSPIRATION BEHIND
THE BLUEPRINT TO EXCELLENCE

Along with modern day concepts on how to lead with quality and character en route to creating a lasting legacy, *The Blueprint to Excellence* incorporates the evidence-based teachings and philosophies of one of the greatest educators who ever lived, Booker T. Washington (1856–1915). This workbook was inspired by two of his books, his bestselling autobiography, *Up from Slavery* and *Character Building*. *Up from Slavery* has been so inspiring and impactful at influencing positive change regardless of a person's ethnic, economic, geographical, or educational background, that it was translated into more than fifteen different languages and has never been out of print.

Born a slave, Washington's life exemplifies how to experience true freedom despite your circumstances. As a former slave, he was able to rise above unimaginable circumstances to become the most influential African American leader of his time. He gained international prominence as a famous educator; and he became the founder of the historic Tuskegee Institute in Alabama, today known as the prestigious Tuskegee University. A significant number of resources indicate that Washington's philosophies for improving the lives of former slaves and their descendants were highly effective. As cited in the book, *Christian Business Legends*, "In 1905 Tuskegee Institute turned out more self-made millionaires than Yale, Harvard, and Princeton universities combined."[1]

Before coming to Alabama, Washington was appointed by the president of Hampton Institute—his alma mater—to educate and advise the American Indian students there. Building on his teaching experience of *the head, the hand, and the heart* from Hampton, he began to lay a foundation which would later become an evidence-based model of how to effectively transform the lives of former slaves and their descendants. This model was instrumental to the success of the school from the time he first opened the doors of Tuskegee on July 4, 1881. It not only transformed lives across cultures, but also across waters—in Haiti, Liberia, and Jamaica, to name a few.

---

1   Rick Williams, Christian Business Legends, Vol. 1, (Business Reform, Publisher, 2004), 37.

As a leader on race relations, Washington gained respect that led to major funding for Tuskegee Institute from some of the nation's wealthiest philanthropists, i.e., Andrew Carnegie, George Eastman, John D. Rockefeller, and Julius Rosenwald. In fact, Rosenwald—who was part owner and president of Sears, Roebuck, and Company—was so inspired by *Up from Slavery*, that the two formed a close relationship which led to their building schools, called Rosenwald Schools, all over the rural south for Blacks who were not being offered an education. Maya Angelou, John Lewis, Medgar Evans, and The Little Rock Nine were among Rosenwald Schools' proud and distinguished graduates. At the time of Washington's death in 1915, there were 78 schools completed or under construction. By the time of Rosenwald's death in 1932, there were more than 5,000 schools, teacher's homes, and training workshops open.

In 1904, a group of Black parents in Laurinburg, North Carolina, wrote to Washington to ask for help in opening a school in their town so their children could receive a quality education. Washington, along with William James Edward—a disciple of Washington's, and incidentally, Spike Lee's great-grandfather—directed Tinny and Emanuel McDuffie, from Snow Hill, Alabama, to open a school maintaining the same principles that Washington established at Tuskegee. At the time of this writing, Laurinburg Institute is one of only four remaining black boarding schools in the country.[1]

After Washington's death in 1915, each succeeding president of Tuskegee upheld Washington's philosophies on education and continued to build on the strong foundation he left. For instance, during the late President Frederick Douglass Patterson's term, due to the school's existing facilities and their engineering and technical instructors, Tuskegee was selected as the training site for the men who later became known as the elite Tuskegee Airmen. These facilities and instructors were in place because of Washington's vision. Today, over 130 years later, the school continues to transform lives, educating thousands upon thousands of great minds in the twenty-first century, under a new generation of leadership.

In *The Negro in Our History*, Carter G. Woodson stated, ". . . history will record that Booker T. Washington, in trying to elevate his oppressed people, so admirably connected education with the practical things of life that he effected such a reform in the education of the world as to place himself in the class with Pestalozzi, Froebel, and Herbart,"[2] German and Swiss philosophers and pioneers of modern education.

---

1   Adam Fairclough, A Class of Their Own: Black Teachers in the Segregated South, (Harvard University Press, Cambridge, Massachusetts, 2007), 212

2   Carter G. Woodson and Charles H. Wesley, ed., The Negro in Our History, 11th Edition, (The Associated Publishers, Inc., Washington, D.C., 1966), 444.

In addition to the above, Washington was advisor to presidents McKinley, Roosevelt, and Taft. He was the first African American to be commemorated on a US fifty-cent coin, and a US postage stamp. He was also the first African American to dine with a president in the White House, which Senator McCain mentioned in his concession speech when he lost the 2008 presidential race—a speech the whole world was listening to as it came upon the election of America's first

Source:www.WhiteHouse.Gov

African American president, Barack Obama. While Booker T. Washington was still alive, US presidents visited the school, and 100 years after his death, in 2015, Michelle Obama, the first African American First Lady of the United States delivered the commencement address. What a legacy!

Senator John and Cindy McCain during 2008
presidential concession speech

Michelle Obama's Commencement Address

Booker Washington and President Theodore Roosevelt at Tuskegee Institute in 1905

ABOUT THE AUTHOR

 **Dr. Sarah Washington O'Neal Rush** is the great-granddaughter of the former slave turned famous educator, and founder of Tuskegee University, Booker T. Washington. She has traveled a long way from her childhood beginnings—from being raised by a single mother, and growing up near poverty in Oakland, California, to becoming an author, speaker, and educator.

Life changed dramatically for her when, as an adult, she discovered the significance of her family history. It happened while visiting Tuskegee University (the school her great-grandfather founded just 16 years after the end of slavery) for the first time. Since then, she's gone from seeking purpose in all the wrong places, to finding it in helping others reach their full potential en route to success. She believes she is living proof that learning about our history and the strength of our bloodline is key to improving life and achieving success. Today, she is considered a living legend by many.

She is the founder of Extraordinary Legacy and Booker T. Washington Excellence Network, (BTWEN). Both of these organizations were created to continue the legacy of her esteemed great-grandfather, as she espouses his evidence-based teachings on character building, education, excellence, leadership, and responsibility. She incorporates his teachings with her modern-day training and her personal and professional experience in mental health and leadership.

She earned a doctorate degree in education in the field of leadership, and a master's degree in the field of psychology. In the field of psychology, she has been an adjunct professor and a clinical counselor, providing therapy to individuals, couples, families, children, and teens. She has provided case management and social work for a foster care home, and she was an administrator for a youth crises shelter. Dr. Rush has published many articles, and has appeared in print media, on radio, on television, on podcasts, and in documentaries discussing mental health, self-improvement, and the historic life and work of her famous great-grandfather.

In addition, she delivers lectures and keynotes around the country. She is the author of *Rising Up from the Blood: A Legacy Reclaimed, A Bridge* Forward and the coauthor of *Timeless Treasures: Reflections of God's Word in the Wisdom of Booker T. Washington*. Both are available on Amazon. com. She also has a published dissertation, *"Exploring the Role of Self-fulfilling Prophesy on the Career Trajectories of Successful African American Adults."* This research explores the lived experiences of successful individuals who grew up in lower socio-economic environments.

Dr. Rush brings a unique perspective and expertise to the table, providing insights and guidance to help navigate the principles and concepts discussed within these pages. Her training in the fields of education, organizational leadership, mental health, and in the nonprofit sector, were instrumental in the development of this book. As well, the tested and proven teachings from her great-grandfather, Booker T. Washington, played a significant role in devising each principle.

About The Blueprint to Excellence

The Blueprint to Excellence is designed to elevate personal and professional growth. Practical and applicable skills, strategies, and techniques are found from the beginning to the end of this book. It is uniquely suited for rising and aspiring leaders, i.e., project leaders, front-line supervisors, managers-in-training, and student leaders. It is also highly recommended for individual influencers, such as educators, coaches, athletes, parents, entrepreneurs, and content creators.

In addition, this book can be a dynamic facilitator's guide for those who serve, teach, or employ rising and aspiring leaders in academic institutions, nonprofit programs, and for-profit businesses. It is particularly appropriate for students in traditional and nontraditional schools, advanced placement programs, and especially higher learning institutions: college and university degree programs, and in trade and vocational schools. Wherever there are rising and aspiring leaders.

The Blueprint to Excellence is written so that it is useful for those who desire to improve beyond what seems possible. As indicated, it is helpful for both individuals and groups. Whether working alone at their own pace, or in partnership with another individual, or working in groups led by facilitators—readers from all walks of life will discover empowering information throughout this workbook that can be applied immediately.

The Blueprint to Excellence uncovers how attitude can impact potential, and thereby, success. The cultivation of positive attitudes is dependent upon a keen sense of *self-awareness* and may require *mindset changes*—two key concepts of this workbook. Thus, the workbook is comprised of sixteen principles, divided into four quadrants—***Being, Growing, Leading, Soaring***— each designed to cultivate skills and qualities of successful attitudes toward personal and professional growth.

Each quadrant contains four principles, along with exercises and assignments. All the principles build upon, intersect, and strengthen each other. They empower individuals to create solid foundations, effectively navigate change, lead by example, and excel through perseverance. They are meant to be revisited as often as needed—whenever a developed skill needs sharpening.

In addition, practical exercises and assignments are provided to enhance understanding and enrich growth. Strength-based, solution-focused, cognitive behavioral, and personality theories inform many of the concepts, exercises, and lessons throughout the book. A wide body of research indicates that these evidence-based theories effectively lead to improved attitudes and behaviors. Hence, ample notetaking and journaling are strongly recommended to reinforce learning. In addition, the material in the appendices provide opportunities to enrich critical skills, including effective communication, writing, time management, interpersonal relationship, and critical thinking skills.

GETTING THE MOST OUT OF THIS WORKBOOK

First and foremost, for the vast majority of the exercises, activities, and assignments, there are no right or wrong answers. They are designed to provoke thought and lead to self-improvement en route to personal and/or professional growth and fulfillment. It's imperative that participants feel free to express their authentic self when completing the lessons—trusting the process. To achieve the most concrete and reflective experience, it is strongly advised to use a dedicated notebook in addition to the journaling pages provided in the workbook.

This is not a "one-and-done" experience. To reinforce learning, the concepts, activities, and exercises should be revisited as often as needed. As we go about our lives we can easily get caught up in negative thinking, distracted by busy days, or become preoccupied in our interpersonal relationships. We may become mentally or emotionally exhausted. We sometimes run on short fuses and quick tempers. When these inevitable circumstances happen, we won't be much good to ourselves—let alone to anyone else. We may lose sight of what is important—faith, family, friends, community, passions, and goals. As you continue to revisit the principles, you will gradually develop sustainable habits that automatically bring you back to positive, constructive, and productive patterns and practices.

Introductions and Appendices

Unlike perhaps some other books, you don't want to skip through the introductory pages in this book. The introductions provide the backdrop for everything presented thereafter. Every introduction has enlightening information—from About Booker T. Washington, to About the Author (his great-granddaughter), to Character Leadership and the Natural Emergence of Ethnic Unity. They will all inspire interest and stimulate the mind.

The appendices are equally as important. They provide a wealth of significant and necessary material for completing the discussions, exercises, activities, and assignments found in the quadrant openings and closings, and throughout the principles. The appendices are packed with an abundance of educational and skill development material—from effective verbal and written communication, to work and life management, to cultivating growth mindsets and self-awareness.

The following worksheets are available online at www.BTWEcellence.com:

- ✓ S.W.O.R. Analysis
- ✓ Four Week Personal Fitness Plan
- ✓ Core Values
- ✓ Debate Evaluation & Score Sheet
- ✓ S.M.A.R.T. Goals

Four Simple Steps to Move Along the Blueprint Most Successfully

Important Note: All of the times listed in parenthesis below are only suggestions for reading, processing, and completing the material, exercises, activities, and assignments. Every individual's or group's journey will be different and should be tailored to meet distinct experiences.

Step One: Read The Sixteen Success Principles Creed (5 minutes)

Before delving in, it's essential to understand the guiding principles that have influenced this work. The "Sixteen Success Principles Creed" at the beginning of this book provides a compass, offering wisdom, insight, and a roadmap to becoming not just better leaders, students, employers, or employees, but better individuals, better human beings.

Step Two: Quadrant Openings (5 minute read; 1 to 3 hours to work through each opening)

Although every opening is important, the first two exercises in Quadrant One are essential to complete. They begin the process of self-discovery and provide a measurement for desired growth.

In *Quadrant One*, in the ***Focus*** section, participants complete a two-part exercise. Part One, ***Connecting the Dots***, begins the process of self-discovery. Part Two, the ***S.W.O.R. Preliminary Analysis***, provides an opportunity to identify a desired area in which to grow and improve, i.e., public speaking, budgeting, eliminating procrastination, gaining self-control.

As a gauge to measure and evaluate progress at the end of the workbook, repeat the analysis with the ***S.W.O.R. Post Analysis***. Or, as an alternative, use the ***S.W.O.R. Post Analysis*** to work on a new area of desired improvement, following the same instructions for the preliminary analysis.

Step Three: The Principles (5 minute read; 2 to 4 hours to work through each principle)

As aforementioned, in the About The Blueprint to Excellence section, each quadrant contains four principles, along with exercises and assignments. All the principles build upon, intersect, and strengthen each other. They empower individuals to create solid foundations, effectively navigate change, lead by example, and excel through perseverance. They are meant to be revisited as often as needed—whenever a developed skill needs sharpening.

Step Four: Quadrant Wrap Ups (5 minute read; 1 to 4 hours to work through each wrap up)

After every four principles is a Quadrant Wrap Up page. They are comprised of **Basic Truths, Activities,** and **Tips** to further solidify the knowledge gained from the principles in each section. This is an excellent place to process and reflect upon the major takeaways from the quadrant.

Symbols used in this workbook:

 Focus Exercises are placed at the beginning of each of the four quadrants. These exercises are intended to get readers to begin thinking about each of the quadrant themes.

 Discussion/Debate Topics, Reflections, and **Assignments** follow each principle. Each of these areas is intended to **provoke thought, generate critical thinking,** and **reinforce concepts.** The *Discussion/Debate Topics* can be used to either generate lively group conversations, or they may be debated using the guidelines in *How to Conduct an Organized Mini Debate* in **Appendix A.**

 Quadrant Wrap Ups are at the end of each quadrant. They cover **Basic Truths, Activities,** and **Tips** to further solidify the knowledge gained from the principles in each section.

 Notes/Journaling is a page that follows each quadrant to capture significant personal experiences that transpire while completing each section of the quadrant. It can also be used to answer exercise and activity questions when more room is needed.

 Rules of Thumb are practical application suggestions and recommendations.

Some Final Thoughts

Each day presents a brand new chance to get it right. We should consciously notice how we are better today than we were yesterday. Perhaps we handled a situation better than we did in the past. Maybe we let a car cut us off while we remained calm. Maybe we moved one step closer to a goal or checked everything off of our to-do list. Maybe we simply drank more water or exercised a little longer. Whatever it may have been, we should acknowledge it. This inspires us to continue to improve daily. Turning these acknowledgements into daily habits prepares us to excel as we go through this workbook.

As well, we should always take time to honor who we are—not in perfection, but in excellence. Someone once described life using an analogy of a snapshot versus a portrait. They said that our lives should not be viewed as snapshots that happen quickly, at the push of a button, without the ability to change once the photo has been taken. Instead, they should be viewed as portraits being painted, adding captivating dimensions and beautiful colors as we grow and improve. We must intentionally take time to do our absolute best to create our unique portrait, fully aware of the process. A portrait that will last long after we're gone—our legacy. One that makes a positive impact and leaves a lasting blueprint for future generations. That is the ultimate intention of *The Blueprint to Excellence.*

INTRODUCTION TO CHARACTER LEADERSHIP

"Character is power. If you want to be powerful in the world, if you want to be strong, influential, and useful, you can be so in no better way than by having strong character."

Booker T. Washington

"Ability may get you to the top, but it takes character to keep you there."

John Wooden

In this book, we develop the concept of Character Leadership—a leadership style which espouses a combination of values and traits rooted in ethics and strength of character. Its foremost objective is to demonstrate genuine interest and appreciation for the well-being of others. Additionally, within the concept of Character Leadership lies this basic reality—before we can effectively lead others, we must be able to effectively lead ourselves. In this sense, whether you are a leader of one, or a leader of many, the tenets of Character Leadership are beneficial for all.

This approach emulates the philosophy of *the head, hand, and heart* model that Booker T. Washington adopted when he opened Tuskegee Institute (Tuskegee University). He first learned of this model as a student at Hampton Institute (Hampton University). The *head* represents knowledge, book smarts, and/or academics. The *hand* represents hard work, and dignity for all types of labor, from the doctor to the janitor. The *heart* represents character strength, giving back, service to others, and for the purposes of this book, ethnic unity.

Character Leadership shares common ground with Servant Leadership, a leadership style pioneered by the late Robert K. Greenleaf. Greenleaf once stated, "The best test as a leader is: Do those served grow as [people]; do they become healthier, wiser, freer, more autonomous, more likely themselves to become leaders?" Similarly, Character Leadership is a leadership approach that empowers followers to evolve into highly ethical future leaders. Its core principles include leading by example, embracing honesty and uprightness, and actively grooming and mentoring others for both present and future success.

As opposed to traditional leadership notions, where the bottom line often takes precedence, both Servant Leadership and Character Leadership prioritize the well-being and growth of their followers. Leaders who practice these styles believe that by putting their followers first—appreciation, loyalty, and motivation will emerge naturally. This, in turn, results in the seamless alignment of organizational vision, mission, goals, and objectives—as a result, the greater good.

To illustrate the profound impact of Character Leadership, the experience and accomplishments of Booker T. Washington are truly inspiring examples. In 1881, a mere 16 years after the abolition of slavery in America, he founded Tuskegee Institute. When the first students arrived, they believed that education would free them from hard work.

However, Washington had a different vision. He understood that hard work was the true path to prosperity. When he led by example, picking up the first axe to clear the forest and build their own structures and farmland, the students' initial protests turned into willing participation.

The result was remarkable: by 1905, Tuskegee had produced more self-made millionaires than Harvard, Princeton, and Yale combined, as documented in "Christian Business Legends."[1]

Character Leadership and the Natural Emergence of Ethnic Unity

"Let's keep before us the fact that, almost without exception, every race or nation that has ever got upon its feet has done so through struggle and trial and persecution; and that out of this very resistance to wrong, out of the struggle against odds, they have gained strength, self-confidence, and experience which they could not have gained in any other way."

Booker T. Washington

Ethnic unity naturally emerges out of the practice of Character Leadership. Thereby, its integration is not only a byproduct, but a critical component of Character Leadership. As the world continues to evolve at an unprecedented pace, blurring boundaries between cultures, the need for a new paradigm of leadership has never been more pressing. Our interconnected global society needs leaders and individuals who can navigate the complexities of a diverse and multicultural world with grace, wisdom, and unwavering integrity.

Ethnic unity greatly enhances the transformative power of character-based leadership. The journey of completing this book will challenge perceptions. It will also encourage the exploration of the potential that manifests when we nurture unity among diverse populations with intentionality.

At the heart of this work lies the recognition that our world is a tapestry woven together by the threads of countless ethnicities, languages, and traditions. Yet, it is in this rich diversity that we often find the signs of discord, misunderstanding, and conflict. Character Leadership grounded in principles of authenticity, empathy, and moral courage, offers a path forward to embracing and celebrating our differences rather than fearing them.

The core values are deeply rooted in the legacy of Booker T. Washington. He was a visionary leader whose life's work embodies the ideals of character strength, as he strived for unity and common ground in extreme adversity and unimaginably harsh conditions. Though he did not realize ethnic unity in its fullness during his lifetime, his journey serves as a powerful testament of how Character Leadership can bridge divides and pave the way for meaningful change.

Following are the descriptions of how the sixteen principles in this workbook build Character Leadership, and naturally lead to the emergence of ethnic unity.

---

1   Rick Williams, Christian Business Legends, Vol. 1, (Business Reform, Publisher, 2004), 37.

Quadrant One: Building on a Foundation of Self-Worth — Being

Principle One: Grounded in a Positive Mind

- Building strong character begins with attaining a positive mindset. When individuals develop a growth mindset, they are more likely to exercise positive thinking, and in turn, character strength. From there, they are more inclined to embrace shared values and appreciate the unique perspectives and strengths that each person brings to the table.

Principle Two: Grounded in a Sound Body

- Physical well-being is intrinsically linked to mental and emotional health. When individuals prioritize their physical health, they are better equipped to engage in open and constructive dialogues about differences. As a result, they can engage in productive conversations that promote understanding, appreciation, and in accordance, unity.

Principle Three: Grounded in Strong Character

- Strong character is the cornerstone of personal/professional development and leadership. This ethical character is critical for building trust within relationships and communities. Individuals with strong character are more likely to bridge divides by demonstrating fairness, integrity, and respect for all.

Principle Four: Grounded in Unshakeable Confidence

- Confidence is a key component of personal/professional development and effective leadership. Those who possess unwavering confidence are less likely to negatively compare themselves with others. As such, they are better equipped to navigate complex issues and conversations with self-assurance, while displaying consideration toward others.

Quadrant Two: Advancing through Change — Growing

Principle Five: Emerging Strength through Trials and Resilience

- Resilience is a biproduct of trials and adversity, and a hallmark of Character Leadership. Individuals who embody resilience are better prepared to confront and address challenges. They can adapt to change, learn from setbacks, and nurture an environment where diversity is seen as an asset rather than an obstacle.

Principle Six: Emerging Self-Agency through Responsibility

- Growth, both personal and professional, requires a sense of responsibility. Those who understand the importance of taking responsibility for their own growth also recognize their role in promoting unity. They become advocates for cooperation and fairness.

Principle Seven: Emerging Solidarity through Healthy Relationships

- Building strong relationships is essential for Character Leadership, as well as for nurturing ethnic unity. Individuals who prioritize relationship building develop networks that span boundaries—creating understanding, empathy, and collaboration.

Principle Eight: Emerging Hope through Faith

- Faith outside of oneself provides inner strength to persevere through challenges. Especially challenges out of our control. Leaders and others who embrace and encourage faith are more likely to smoothly transcend beyond adversity, conflict, and division.

Quadrant Three: Leading by Example — Leading

Principle Nine: Elevating Legacy through Vision

- Rather than seeing circumstances as they are, visionaries see them as what they could be. Advancing the vision plays a critical role in promoting the best in all people. Consequently, enriching unity through shared goals and aspirations.

Principle Ten: Elevating Knowledge through Education

- Education is a powerful tool for rising above challenges and bridging divides. Leaders and others who advocate education empower individuals from all backgrounds to reach their full potential. Thus, contributing to the greater good in society.

Principle Eleven: Elevating Dignity through Work

- Those who honor the dignity of labor recognize the worth of every individual, regardless of their title, credentials, or background. This principle advances fairness and promotes the merging of ideas. These are key elements of fostering unity.

Principle Twelve: Elevating Wealth through Financial Responsibly

- Character Leadership promotes responsible financial management. When financial responsibility is modeled, a fundamental example is set for others to follow. Accordingly, this helps to reduce economic disparities that can hinder unity.

Quadrant Four: Excelling in Perseverance — Soaring

Principle Thirteen: The Power of Gratitude

- Gratitude is a powerful character building tool. Leaders and others who practice gratitude are more likely to appreciate individual contributions. This appreciation lays the foundation for mutual respect and unity.

Principle Fourteen: The Power of Purpose

- Individuals who discover their purpose find fulfillment. When they align their purpose with their passion, their determination to live out their purpose increases. With that, they are better equipped to understand how their purpose fits in with the bigger picture of unity.

Principle Fifteen: The Power of Service

- Service is a fundamental aspect of Character Leadership. Individuals who prioritize service create a sense of community and interconnectedness that prevails over divisions, hardships, and selfish ambition. Once all of the other principles are mastered, the ability to serve can be performed wholeheartedly, and at the highest level.

Principle Sixteen: The Power of Excellence

- Individuals who strive for excellence set high standards for themselves and others. This commitment to excellence transcends ethnic boundaries, promoting a culture of continuous improvement and collaboration. When each of the preceding principles are put into practice, the final product is the natural emergence of excellence.

From the above list of descriptions of each principle, it becomes clear that Character Leadership is not only a powerful approach to personal and professional development, but it's also inherently linked to the promotion of respect, connection, and understanding. Accordingly, through these principles and practices, we become catalysts for positive improvement in our institutions, organizations, communities, and beyond.

In conclusion, Character Leadership, including how it invokes ethnic unity, is not a mere concept. Rather, it's a phenomenal approach to shaping a brighter future. The insights gained through this book will lead to the development of well-prepared individuals, students, professionals, and leaders. Those who lead by example in the celebration of unity, inspiring shared values, and leaving a legacy of lasting positive change.

PREPARE TO BE...

By the end of the first quadrant, you will become sound in awareness of how *mind*, *body*, *character*, and *confidence* play a pivotal role in being prepared for success. You will have mastered the first four out of the sixteen success principles embodied in the concept of *being*. You will also begin to uncover what it takes to move on to the next level of *growing*.

QUADRANT ONE: BUILDING ON A FOUNDATION OF SELF-WORTH – CULTIVATING AN ATTITUDE OF

"The individual who puts the most into life is the individual who gets the most out of life."

There is a reason we are called *human beings* and not *human doings*. Before we can *do* anything well for anyone else, we must first be unfaltering about *being* well within ourselves. In fact, it is not only improbable, but arguably impossible to effectively lead, guide, influence, or help others when we have not properly attended to ourselves. Thus, continuous personal growth is non-negotiable. It's in this very essence of being that the foundations of leadership, character, and unity are laid.

Within Quadrant One, we emphasize self-discovery and self-improvement. In actualizing this personal growth, attitude adjustments are often all it takes to become the best version of ourselves. It may be as simple as breaking a habit that can hinder a positive mindset. For instance, instead of saying, "I have to," start saying, "I get to." This small act can reap enormous benefits in perspective.

Quadrant One encapsulates four pivotal principles that form the bedrock of self-worth: A positive **mind**, a sound **body**, strong **character**, and enduring **confidence** are the foundation of healthy and unshakeable **self-worth**. When we possess this kind of self-worth, we experience the essence of what it means to be free from the weight of inadequacy and negativity. Possession begins in the mind—with a commitment to continuous self-development and improvement.

 **FOCUS EXERCISE:**

Part One: Connecting the Dots

Thoughtfully answer the questions in the four boxes on the next page to gain insight into how you may have arrived at the level of self-worth you experience today (high, medium, low).

For a deeper experience, use a dedicated notebook to write down your responses.

Looking back on your life. . .

1. List five to ten defining events *Example 1: Parent's divorce.* *Example 2: Moving to a new neighborhood.* *Example 3: Coming in 1st place in a track meet.*	**4. List three to five pivotal lessons learned** *Example 1: Who I hang out with matters.* *Example 2: Actions have consequences.* *Example 3: Commitment pays off.*
2. List five to seven significant choices *Example 1: Pushing through during a difficulty.* *Example 2: Giving up during a difficulty.* *Example 3: Choosing to take a hard course.*	**3. List three to five key people** *Example 1: First grade teacher.* *Example 2: Childhood neighbor.* *Example 3: Grandfather.*

Part Two: S.W.O.R. Preliminary Analysis

Complete the *S.W.O.R. Preliminary Analysis* in Appendix B. This will be the first of two times that you will complete this analysis. The next time will be in *Quadrant Four Wrap Up* when you complete the *S.W.O.R. Post Analysis*. The post analysis provides a gauge for your progress by the end of this program.

Instructions for completing the *S.W.O.R. Analysis*:

S.W.O.R. Preliminary Analysis: (Complete prior to beginning *Success Principle 1*)

1. Write down an area where you have a strong desire to grow and improve.

2. With the area in mind, brainstorm brief answers to the questions under *Self-Assurance, Worries, Options, and Risks/Rewards/Readiness* using the four corresponding boxes on page two of the analysis.

3. After you've completed all three pages of the analysis, come back to page one, and answer the scaling question at the bottom of the page. If the number is less than 10, consider what it would take for you to move up by 1, 2, 3. . . If the number is more than 1, consider why it isn't lower? Write down your thoughts in a dedicated notebook.

4. You will complete the *S.W.O.R. Post Analysis* in *Quadrant Four Wrap Up*. See instructions below.

S.W.O.R. Post Analysis: (Complete in *Quadrant Four Wrap Up*)

1. Follow the instructions above for numbers 1 and 2 using the same area for growth and improvement that you chose in the preliminary analysis. This provides a gauge to measure and evaluate progress that occurred between preliminary and post analysis.

Or

2. As an alternative, you may choose to work on a new desired area of improvement in the post analysis, following the same instructions for the preliminary analysis.

Note: These blank forms may be copied to use anytime you desire to work on improvement in any area of your life or work. They may also be found on the website: www.BTWExcellence.com.

Success Principle 1 ~ Grounded in a Positive Mind

"It is not possible to improve the condition in any race until the mind is awakened and improved."

No matter where we are in life, there is always room for growth and improvement. One of the most common areas is in erasing negative thoughts from our mind. These are thoughts that only serve to keep us stuck, such as, *I can't, I should have, Why me,* and, *If only.* Thoughts lead to words, words lead to feelings, and feelings lead to actions. Hence, to prevent these thoughts, we must stay aware of how we talk to ourselves. If we continually dwell on the negative, we can't realize the power that positive thinking draws out. Our adversaries (e.g., haters, enemies) can then relax, satisfied that they don't have to lift a finger to complicate our lives, because we would be doing that on our own.

We must also be cautious of messages we allow in from the outside. All our lives we receive suggestive messages from others. Some positive, some negative. Some of the most influential messages come from parents, peers, teachers, celebrities, advertisements, music, television, and social media. We're bombarded with these messages all day long. They operate much like the *law of suggestion* and may lead to *self-fulfilling prophecy.* They have the potential to shape our beliefs, traditions, politics, and even our life's purpose. They can be destructive if used to control, manipulate, or cripple individuality. They can also be positive when delivered with good intention. An example of the latter is receiving constructive criticism from someone who has our best interest at heart.

We harness the power of Principle One by cultivating a positive mindset that empowers us to awaken the best within ourselves and, in turn, contribute to the growth and unity of our diverse world. In the vast sea of opinions and influences, we must remember that we can only control ourselves. We can't control others. We must be careful not to get swayed by or swept up into their stuff. We must not let their issues become our issues, or their thoughts become our thoughts. This leads to the absence of *critical thinking*, and the presence of *groupthink.* To avoid this, we must become vigilant truth-seekers, making informed decisions based on careful assessment of facts, opinions, and our inner wisdom.

Discussion/Debate Topics

☐ Review Quadrant One Focus Exercise, Connecting the Dots.

☐ Why is it important to be aware of how the power of suggestion influences behavior? (Refer to *Critical Thinking* and *Groupthink* in Appendix A, and *Self-fulfilling Prophecy and the Law of Suggestion* and *Mindset Awareness* in Appendix C.)

☐ How do thoughts, feelings, and actions impact behavior? (Refer to *Reversing Irrational Thoughts, Changing Negative Behaviors* in Appendix C.)

Self-Reflection (use the journaling page or a dedicated notebook for your answers).

o Refer to the *Mindset Chart* in Appendix C to locate which side of the chart you identify most closely with. What is the evidence of this?

o Reflect on your responses to the Connecting the Dots exercise in Quadrant One opening. Were any significant insights made? If so, consider how that information may be helpful for your growth and development moving forward.

Assignment: Getting the Most out of this Principle

o Throughout the week, pay close attention to your self-talk. When you catch yourself speaking negatively about yourself (or others), stop and change your words to constructive words. For example, instead of saying, "I messed up!" reframe by saying, "I made a mistake. What's the lesson?" Or, instead of saying "I have to" say "I get to." (Refer to *Reframing Negative Self-Talk into Positive Self-Affirmations* in Appendix C.) Write down as many examples as you can and be prepared to discuss.

Success Principle 2 ~ Grounded in a Sound Body

"The first prerequisite for making life effective for oneself or society is a sound body."

Despite the reoccurrence of various medical pandemics (i.e., the Spanish flu; HIV/Aids; SARS; Swine flu; Ebola; and Covid19) we are fortunate to have been born in this day and age. With medical research advancing around the globe and improvements being made, we are living longer. However, as we strive for longevity, we must not overlook the paramount importance of quality in our daily living. It helps if we view our bodies as rare and priceless entities that enfold our heart, our mind, and our soul. Therefore, just as we are careful about what goes into our minds, we must also be careful about how we take care of our bodies.

Take time to learn and keep up with the studies about what's healthy for your body, and what's not. For example, over many years, countless studies continue to show that drinking plenty of water can improve our health in many ways. These include maintaining healthy skin, preventing certain cancers, and helping our digestive system function properly. Studies also consistently find that eating plenty of fruits and vegetables, along with regular physical exercise helps to prevent heart attacks, diabetes, and stroke, and leads to emotional wellbeing. Conversely, a wide body of research also indicates that too much of anything can be bad for health. Especially when it comes to alcohol, sugar, fried foods, and certain carbohydrates.

Ideally, even the healthiest individuals should make it a practice to include preventative measures in their self-care plan. According to medical experts, scheduling regular physical exams can create a health baseline and maximize wellness. Some advise the following: healthy teens should have a physical once a year; young adults in their twenties should have one every two or three years; adults in their thirties and forties, every other year; and once a year again, beginning at age fifty.

Principle Two encourages the exploration of best practices for maintaining optimal physical health. Visit local health fairs, libraries, and listen to trusted television and radio programs, podcasts, or YouTube videos that cater to good health. Today, there's little excuse for not being aware of what leads to a quality of life.

Note: No content in this book should ever be used as a substitute for direct medical advice from your doctor or other qualified clinician.

Discussion/Debate Topics

☐ Review the Self-Reflection and Assignment from Success Principle 1.

☐ What are some of the advantages of maintaining physical wellness?

☐ Why do different cultures and ethnicities experience health issues differently?

Self-Reflection (use the journaling page or a dedicated notebook for your answers).

o What are at least three things you can incorporate immediately towards your long-term goals for physical wellness?

Assignment: Getting the Most out of this Principle

o After conducting research, write a 250-500 word double-spaced essay on the essential body parts for healthy living, (e.g., heart, liver, kidneys, colon). Include how they work, and preventative measures to keep them working optimally. (Refer to *Simple Steps to Developing an Effective Essay* in Appendix A.)

o Refer to the *Four-Week Personal Fitness Plan* in Appendix B to develop a fitness plan. Include exercise and nutrition.

Success Principle 3 ~ Grounded in Strong Character

"Character, not circumstances, makes the man."

A notable quote from Dr. Martin Luther King, Jr. is, *"I have a dream that someday my children will not be judged by the color of their skin, but by the content of their character."* Another notable quote, from Coach John Wooden, *"Ability may take you to the top, but it takes character to keep you there."* A fundamental feature of good character is commitment to keeping our word. Another crucial feature is what we do when no one is looking. Demonstrating good character must be consistent. It's easy to maintain it when our circumstances fall into place and lose it when they don't. But it's in the latter circumstance that strong character is truly demonstrated.

Strong character doesn't happen accidentally. It happens with intentionality. We build and strengthen character by consistently practicing patience, kindness, and self-control. It's important to remember that to develop strength in these areas, our circumstances must be tested. We will know that we're achieving our goal each time we pass the test. The more we pass, the stronger we become. If we fail from time to time, we acknowledge our shortcomings and continue the work—never giving up and never giving in. When we stand resolute in the face of adversity, when we extend compassion to those who may differ from us, and when we exercise self-control in the midst of turmoil, we are demonstrating strong character.

In embracing Principle Three, we recognize that our character is not merely a personal attribute; it is a bridge that connects us to others. It transcends the boundaries of race and ethnicity, fostering a shared commitment to fairness, respect, and integrity. By strengthening our character, we contribute to the groundwork upon which more united and harmonious alliances can be established with others.

Discussion/Debate Topics

☐ Review the Self-Reflection and Assignment from Success Principle 2.

☐ Why is it so important to keep our word?

☐ What can we do to ensure that we are getting and giving respect?

☐ Is social etiquette necessary today? Why or why not? (Refer to *Netiquette: Effective Communication Online* in Appendix A.)

Self-Reflection (use the journaling page or a dedicated notebook for your answers).

o Who is someone (living, deceased, famous, or not) in your opinion, who consistently exercises high moral character? Briefly explain why you chose that person.

o List at least three positive characteristics you possess, or desire to possess, that are similar to the characteristics of the person you named above. Write a **D** after the characteristic if it is a desire, and a **P** if you already possess the characteristic.

Assignment: Getting the Most out of this Principle

o Complete *Core Values Exercise* in Appendix B.

o Throughout the week, observe when you see mutual respect occurring between two or more people, or between you and someone else.

Success Principle 4 ~ Grounded in Confidence

"I will never allow any man to drag me down so low as to make me hate him."

Confidence is not an acquired trait; it's our birthright. Yet, as we journey through life, many of us lose sight of this inherent gift. Studies show about 85 percent of two-year-olds have high levels of confidence. As they age, they begin to believe they are who others tell them they are. For example, "good" or "bad." At age 12, the confidence level drops to about 50 percent. This is commonly the result of how others treat (or mistreat) them. At this age, children are very impressionable. By age 15, studies show that confidence tumbles to around 5 percent. This is in line with how we begin to self-sabotage as we compare ourselves to others and become more concerned about what they think of us. By the time we reach adulthood, the number climbs back up to one in three adults experiencing high levels of confidence, indicating that regaining confidence takes work.

As children, unfortunately we are not able to do much about how our spirits may get broken and our confidence gets stripped away. But as we get older, having confidence is a matter of taking responsibility to regain it. An excellent place to begin is by looking at our ancestry. Here we can learn of, or reacquaint ourselves with, the struggles, perseverance, resilience, and victories of our bloodline. This can provide encouragement in a way that nothing else can. As this occurs, our individual worth increases, and we no longer have the need to compare ourselves to others, nor do we continue to dwell on what they may be thinking about us.

Principle Four implores us to stand up for ourselves without violating others, and uplift others without tearing anyone else down. In this sense, confidence is a requirement for maintaining healthy relationships. Often it is insecurities that cause relationships to break down. As we embrace this, we acknowledge that confidence is not just a personal attribute; it is a beacon that guides us toward self-discovery, self-acceptance, and the capacity to inspire unity by celebrating the diversity of the human experience.

The charts below show physiological differences in those who feel good about who they are, and those who have little confidence. The following two boxes provide examples of these differences:

Box 1: Physiological effects of an individual with low levels of self-confidence:	Box 2: Physiological effects of an individual with high levels of self-confidence:
Sitting: slouched posture	**Sitting:** straight up or leaning forward
Face: slack and lifeless	**Face:** upward
Breathing: shallow and short	**Breathing:** deliberate and full
Eyes: downward, avoids eye contact	**Eyes:** upward, welcomes eye contact
Head and Shoulders: down and slumped	**Head and Shoulders:** up and back

Discussion/Debate Topics

☐ Review the Self-Reflection and Assignment from Success Principle 3.

☐ How does a small child begin to show confidence?

☐ What might happen to cause a child to lose confidence?

Self-Reflection (use the journaling page or a dedicated notebook for your answers).

o Briefly describe a time when you demonstrated a high level of confidence.

Assignment: Getting the Most out of this Principle

o Throughout the week pay close attention to when you fall into any of the physiological positions in Box 1, then immediately incorporate the physiological positions in Box 2.

o Prepare a presentation on an area of the program that has made an impact on you thus far. Make it adequate for delivering a three to five minute oral presentation. During the week, practice delivering it orally. (Refer to *Public Speaking Skills: How to Communicate with Confidence* in Appendix A.)

Being...

Quadrant One Wrap Up ~ Building on a Foundation of Self-Worth

Basic Truths of Healthy Self-Worth:

➢ We can't sufficiently love others until we first learn to love ourselves properly.

➢ Healthy self-talk, self-respect, and self-awareness are all non-negotiable.

➢ Positive self-talk promotes a strong mind.

➢ Our bodies are rare and priceless entities that enfold our heart, mind, and soul.

➢ Confidence is our birthright.

➢ Ability may take you to the top, but strength of character keeps you there.

Quadrant One Activities

1. List 3 to 5 reasons why there is a stigma associated with receiving mental health counseling.

2. Explain delayed and instant gratification as they relate to mindfulness and mindlessness.

3. Research how you got your first name and the significance of your name.

4. Research significant events that took place in history on or around your birth date.

5. Refer to *Tracing Your Genealogy* in Appendix C to learn how to uncover your ancestry.

10 Tips for Maintaining Healthy Self-Worth

✓ Pay attention to what you say when you talk to yourself.

✓ Never compare yourself, your family, or your achievements to anyone else.

✓ Surround yourself with people who make you feel good about who you are.

✓ Surround yourself with people who have healthy self-love/self-esteem/self-respect.

✓ Accept, embrace, and respect everything about yourself.

✓ Work on areas where you want to improve.

✓ Acknowledge areas in your life that you are happy with.

✓ Always forgive yourself for your mistakes and turn them into lessons.

✓ Remember, "NO" is a complete sentence; use it to protect your worth and integrity.

✓ Learn about your ancestry to discover where traits of your inner strength come from.

Use the following page for self-reflections, notes, and to journal about your experience in Quadrant One.

![pencil icon] **Notes/Journaling**

_____

_____

_____

_____

_____

_____

_____

_____

_____

_____

_____

_____

_____

_____

_____

_____

_____

_____

> **Rule of Thumb**: Intentionally cancel out negative thoughts by replacing them with positive ones. Negative thoughts are toxic. They will inevitably eat away at your spirit.

PREPARE TO GROW

By the end of the second quadrant, you will become sound in the awareness of how *trials and resilience, responsibility, relationships,* and *faith* play key roles in your ability to continue to grow in success. You will have mastered eight of the sixteen success principles embodied in the concepts of *being* and *growing*. You will also begin to uncover what it takes to move on to the next level of *leading*.

QUADRANT TWO ~ MANAGING THROUGH CHANGE

CULTIVATING AN ATTITUDE OF

"It is only through the surmounting of difficulties that individuals are made powerful."

There is a saying, *"Life is what happens while we're busy making other plans."* Successfully managing through circumstances of change is about skillfully navigating through those unexpected, undesired detours. The good news is that the most difficult circumstances are breeding ground for the most meaningful and sustainable growth. Having the right perspective during disruptions leads to victory on the other side.

The combination of *trials and resilience*; taking *responsibility* to rise above adversity; decerning which *relationships* are healthy, and which are toxic along the way; and possessing invincible *faith* through it all, goes a long way in producing steadfast personal and professional growth and fulfillment—the kind of growth and fulfillment that cannot be easily dismantled.

Quadrant Two addresses the deeper meaning of change. In other words, it goes beneath the surface of what meets the eye to get to the greater possibilities of what lies ahead. Often, it is in change that we find silver linings, blessings in disguise, and new potential.

 FOCUS EXERCISE:

Guest of Honor

1. Imagine that you are the guest of honor at an awards ceremony. You can only invite five people. Who will those five people be?

    ➢ What are you receiving the award for?

    ➢ During the event, a select group of people are going to reflect on your life. What would you like them to share about you?

2. Brainstorm how you can accomplish what you want them to share?

For a deeper experience, use a dedicated notebook to write down your responses.

Success Principle 5 ~ Emerging Strength Through Trials and Resilience

"It often requires more courage to suffer in silence than to rebel, more courage not to strike back than to retaliate, more courage to be silent than to speak."

Trials are an inescapable part of the human experience. It has been said that at any given point in time, *"we are either in a storm, just coming out of a storm, or headed towards one."* They come to us in various forms, testing the very core of our character. Yet, it is not the trial itself that defines us; it is our response to it, our unwavering courage in the face of adversity. It's what creates resilience. Our choice in our response will determine whether we come out weak or strong, powerless or powerful. There is another saying that goes, *"you can be pitiful or powerful, but you can't be both."*

It takes courage to wait, put our emotions aside, and then respond with tact, logic, and sensibility. However, if we keep dwelling on the trial, thinking about it and talking about it, the negative noise will drown out the positive lessons which the trial came to teach. These lessons can guide us through future difficulties, enable us to avoid similar ones, and give us wisdom to teach others. Thus, instead of asking "Why me?" ask, "What am I going to do about it?" To do otherwise impedes our path toward resilience.

On a positive note, trials are often temporary, and always opportunities for growth. Some of them we'll have control over, while others will be out of our control. To end up better after coming out than we were going in, we can't wait until there is a problem to frantically seek a solution. Instead, we must anchor our tent during the calm before the storm, by making a practice of integrating mindfulness exercises in our daily routine. Soon, healthy solutions will begin to transpire, becoming second nature, occurring naturally when we need them most.

Within Principle Five, we discover the power of courage. The courage to endure, the courage to learn, and the courage to emerge from trials. Not only as stronger individuals but also as students, workers, and leaders capable of guiding diverse communities through their own storms with empathy, wisdom, and strength.

Discussion/Debate Topics

- ☐ Review Quadrant One Wrap Up Activities and Quadrant Two Focus Exercise.

- ☐ Review the Self-Reflection and Assignment from Success Principle 4.

- ☐ How might you explain why bad things happen to good people?

- ☐ How do we determine what is in or out of our control in terms of resolving difficulties?

- ☐ What are some mindfulness techniques that may be useful in the midst of a trial that you can practice when life is going well? (Refer to *Mindfulness Meditations* in Appendix C).

Self-Reflection (use the journaling page or a dedicated notebook for your answers).

- o Think about a difficulty that impacted you and describe a lesson that was (or could have been) learned.

Assignment: Getting the Most out of this Principle

- o The next time you are the driver or passenger in a car during a traffic jam, or when other drivers are being rude or irate, or going too fast or slow, practice techniques to keep yourself calm. (e.g., deep breathing, patience, delayed gratification).

- o Write a 500–750 word double-spaced essay describing a trial you've faced that took courage to overcome. Include the following: working backwards, first describe key events that led up to the trial; followed by steps you took to get through it; then what you would do differently if you had to face it again; what you feel worked well; how you felt once you were on the other side of the trial; and lessons learned. (Refer to *Simple Steps to Developing an Effective Essay* in Appendix A.)

Success Principle 6 ~ Emerging Self-agency through Responsibility

*"Let us hold up our head, and with firm and steady tread go manfully forward.
No one likes to feel that he is continually following a funeral procession."*

In the grand scheme of things, taking responsibility for our actions, decisions, and responses is the hallmark of true agency. Taking responsibility for what we can control relieves us from getting caught up in feelings of anger, bitterness, and defeat. As the saying goes, harboring those types of feelings is like *"taking poison, and hoping your enemy will die."* When we blame someone or something outside of ourselves (i.e., manager, coworker, teacher, parent) for our circumstances, we strip ourselves of the power to do anything about them. Of course, there will always be instances when situations are caused by others, and are simply out of our control. But even in the most challenging circumstances, we can take responsibility to seek a solution and/or discover a silver lining.

To be okay with accepting responsibility, our self-worth must be strong and intact. As alluded to in the principle on self-worth, when we do not carefully tend to ourselves daily, our self-worth diminishes. This can be especially true when others tamper with it. As a result, we may begin to hold them responsible, hoping they will "fix us," or "fix it," giving our power over to them. In this case, the silver lining is that once we take responsibility to control the only person we can—ourselves—the damage is never irreversible. We can take our power back. From that point, there is nothing that can block our progress.

By embracing Principle Six, we not only cultivate self-agency but lay an inspiring path for others to follow. We demonstrate that true power lies not in pointing fingers but in taking action, in choosing to hold our heads high and stride forward with purpose and determination.

Discussion/Debate Topics

- ☐ Review the Self-Reflection and Assignment from Success Principle 5,

- ☐ Discuss the pros and cons of blaming versus taking responsibility.

- ☐ What are examples of silver linings in the midst of difficulties?

Self-Reflection (use the journaling page or a dedicated notebook for your answers).

- o Think of a negative circumstance you experienced due to someone else's choices or behaviors. Describe how you could have resolved it even though you weren't at fault.

Assignment: Getting the Most out of this Principle

- o Write your personal mission statement. It should be a living statement that will evolve and change as you continue an endless journey of growth, improvement, and self-discovery. (Refer to *Crafting a Personal Mission Statement* in Appendix B.)

Success Principle 7 ~ Emerging Solidarity through Healthy Relationships

"If there is any good in a person, let us seek to find it; the evil will take care of itself."

We need relationships to thrive. We need relationships for solidarity and stability. We are much stronger together—finding common ground—than we are when we are divided. Therefore, to develop and maintain healthy relationships we must always meet people where they are, not where we want them to be, or think they should be. We never know what someone is going through at any given moment, or what they have gone through in their lifetime. Remember, no one is flawless. For every flaw we find in someone else, they can match us one for one. Just a different flaw, and likely one they don't have, or notice, within themselves.

Relationships come in many forms—intimate, familial, friendly, collegial, and more. There will be times when we need to let go of certain relationships to thrive. Instead of holding on to a bad relationship, let it go before bitterness, hatred, or anger begin to creep in and eventually take over. A wise rule of thumb is, if the good outweighs the bad, keep the relationship, but if the bad outweighs the good, or even comes close, it is time to reevaluate the necessity of that relationship in your life. Never hold on to what's holding you back.

Principle Seven explores the art of nurturing relationships that foster solidarity and celebrate the richness of diversity. As individuals, students, professionals, and/or leaders, it is our duty to recognize the intrinsic worth of every individual and the unique perspective they bring to our shared journey.

Discussion/Debate Topics

- ☐ Review the Self-Reflection and Assignment from Success Principle 6.

- ☐ How might understanding the functions of the id, ego, and superego be helpful? (Refer to *Personality—Id, Ego, and Superego* in Appendix C.)

- ☐ When might defense mechanisms be necessary? (Refer to *Personality—Common Defense Mechanisms* in Appendix C.)

- ☐ Do you have close relationships with anyone outside of your culture, ethnicity, or race? If yes, how has it impacted your life? If not, why do you believe that is?

- ☐ What are some of the emotional impacts of pressure (e.g., from a peer, boyfriend/girlfriend, family, parent(s), teacher, and/or supervisor), and what are some effective coping skills to counteract the negative impacts?

Self-Reflection (use the journaling page or a dedicated notebook for your answers).

- o What is the most important relationship in your life? Why? Has it made you stronger? If so, how?

Assignment: Getting the Most out of this Principle

- o Write a 250–500 word double-spaced essay on a challenging relationship (current or past). Discuss whether it is a necessary relationship, and how you might resolve the difficulties, by either dissolving or improving the relationship. (Refer to *Simple Steps to Developing an Effective Essay* in Appendix A.)

Success Principle 8 ~ Emerging Hope through Faith

"I was awakened by my mother kneeling over her children and fervently praying."

Faith is having a strong belief that there is more to life than what meets the eye. People of all different faiths have one thing in common: a strong conviction that no matter how dismal problems may appear, something greater is taking place. Faith is what pushes people beyond their limits. It moves people from addiction to recovery. It motivates them from complacency to embracing a higher cause. It changes people from the inside out. When we lack faith, we are more likely to experience stress, anger, depression, and frustration, which may render us hopeless and helpless. The opposite of hopelessness and helplessness is faith.

When circumstances seem too much to endure, faith makes all the difference. When situations are out of our control (death, disease, natural disasters), we can turn to faith. Having faith makes the most sense when nothing else does. When we exercise faith daily, our life experiences a transformation process—moving from less doubt, worry, and confusion to more peace, ingenuity, and freedom. As our challenges become lighter, our outlook becomes brighter, and solutions become easier to find.

Principle Eight offers insight for inner peace, even in the midst of turmoil. It's not meant for us to carry the burdens of this imperfect world on our shoulders alone. It's impossible. We are only responsible for our small part in this huge universe—that's our life's purpose. When we attempt more than that, inner turmoil may ensue. But with faith we can restore order to our lives.

Discussion/Debate Topics

☐ Review the Self-Reflection and Assignment from Success Principle 7.

☐ How might exercising faith help you make it through a difficult circumstance?

☐ Is there such a thing as a miracle? How do you explain a miracle versus a coincidence?

Self-Reflection (use the journaling page or a dedicated notebook for your answers).

o If you had no fear of failure or rejection, what is something you would attempt?

o Imagine taking a leap of faith and attempting that thing. What's the worst thing that could happen?

Assignment: Getting the Most out of this Principle

o Research the ancient and modern lists of the Seven Wonders of the World. Ponder one or two that speak the loudest to you personally. Journal your thoughts.

o Write a 250–500 word double-spaced essay on what faith means to you. (Refer to *Simple Steps to Developing an Effective Essay* in Appendix A.)

o Prepare a presentation on an area of the program that has made an impact on you thus far. Make it adequate for delivering a three to five minute oral presentation. During the week, practice delivering it orally. (Refer to *Public Speaking Skills: How to Communicate with Confidence* in Appendix A.)

$\checkmark$ Growing...

Quadrant Two Wrap Up ~ Managing Through Change

Basic Truths of Change Management:

➤ The only thing constant is change.

➤ Resilience comes through trials—creating opportunities for growth.

➤ Prepare for the storms of life during the calm periods.

➤ Some relationships last forever, others last for a season.

➤ Each day presents a new opportunity to grow, improve, and get it right.

➤ Faith restores hope in the midst of hardship.

Quadrant Two Activities

1. Read about I-Statements (Refer to *Mastering the Art of Using I-Statements* in Appendix A.)

2. Complete Perception Exercise (Refer to *Personality and Perception* in Appendix C.)

10 Tips for staying positive in the midst of change

✓ Never become complacent with the status quo.

✓ Stay abreast of change instead of getting lost in it.

✓ Respond, instead of reacting, to challenges presented by change.

✓ Rely on past skills to make it through present challenges.

✓ Learn and practice coping skills before you need to use them.

✓ Recognize whether situations are either in or out of your control.

✓ Take advantage of new learning opportunities presented by a changed situation.

✓ We determine whether to have a positive or negative attitude in the midst of change.

✓ Developing grit and true courage requires interaction with difficulties, so embrace them.

✓ Before confronting someone with a problem, have at least three solutions ready to bring to the table.

Use the following page for self-reflections, notes, and to journal about your experience in Quadrant Two.

![Notes/Journaling icon] **Notes/Journaling**

_____

_____

_____

_____

_____

_____

_____

_____

_____

_____

_____

_____

_____

_____

_____

_____

_____

_____

_____

Rule of thumb: Sometimes others just need someone to listen— if you're not asked a question, don't offer a suggestion.

PREPARE TO LEAD...

By the end of the third quadrant, you will become sound in awareness of how ***vision, education, dignity of work, and financial responsibility*** play a significant role in rising to success. You will have mastered twelve of the sixteen success principles embodied in the concepts of ***being, growing, and leading.*** You will also begin to uncover what it takes to move on to the next level of Soaring.

QUADRANT THREE ~ LEADING BY EXAMPLE

CULTIVATING AN ATTITUDE OF

"One cannot hold another down in a ditch without staying down in the ditch with him."

In the realm of Character Leadership, we must think like a leader even when there is no one to lead but ourselves. However, even if just one person is following you, looking up to you, or seeking guidance from you, consider yourself a leader. You may experience this at work, home, school, or in the community. As such, it's important to know that others are watching you. The best leaders welcome this. They choose to lead by example. They raise and set the bar high while showing others how to reach it, and then surpass it.

Great leaders view leadership as an opportunity to groom others to become leaders. They consider themselves role models and set standards of excellence. They set examples by staying focused on their *vision*, sharpening their skills through continuous *education*, performing their *work* with dignity and integrity, and followed by demonstrating *financial responsibility* with their earnings.

In Quadrant Three, we acknowledge that every step we take, every decision we make, and every action we choose has the power to inspire Character Leadership. Not only in us, but also in those who walk behind us, alongside us, and even ahead of us. Simply put, we recognize that we have the potential to make a positive impact within our own lives, as well as in the lives of everyone around us.

 Focus Exercise:

Leadership Qualities

1. Who are three people whom you admire for their leadership qualities? What do you admire about them?

2. Where do you recognize those qualities in yourself?

3. Name at least three environments (i.e., work, school, home, community) where you can practice effective leadership skills?

4. Name at least three areas where you can sharpen and practice leadership skills, e.g., communication, role modeling, innovation, giving constructive feedback, team building.

For a deeper experience, use a dedicated notebook to write down your responses.

Success Principle 9 ~ Elevating Legacy through Vision

"The future is built on the materials of the past."

A strong legacy that will live on long after we're gone begins with *vision*, *dedication*, and *commitment*. Booker T. Washington mastered all three. With very little financial resources and unimaginable racism surrounding him, he was willing to stand against all odds, as he looked beyond what was, and saw what could be. Because he stood, thousands of schools, community centers, streets, and even neighborhoods are named after him to honor his legacy. And because of his unwavering focus, Tuskegee University still stands strong today. ***That's vision.***

In the face of adversity, he never swayed from his vision to uplift the people in the South. On July 4, 1881, he opened Tuskegee Institute in an old, dilapidated church. He borrowed money to purchase an abandoned plantation surrounded by heaps of seemingly endless brush, weeds, and trees, which he and his students cleared to improve the land. They built a kiln and made bricks to build additional buildings. They built more classrooms, a dining hall, a dormitory, and a chapel. ***That's dedication.***

While in New York raising funds for Tuskegee, Booker T. Washington became terminally ill. With only days to live, he summoned his wife to come get him. From his hospital bed he said, *"I was born in the South, I lived and worked in the South, and I plan to die in the South."* His wife brought him back home to Alabama, where he died the next day, in the South. ***That's commitment.***

In Principle Nine, we delve into the significance of crafting a compelling vision. A vision that not only guides our actions but also becomes a source of light and inspiration for others. This is the kind of vision that sets the stage for creating a great and lasting legacy.

Discussion / Debate Topics

☐ Review Quadrant Two Wrap Up Activities and Quadrant Three Focus Exercise.

☐ Review the Self-Reflection and Assignment from Success Principle 8.

☐ Discuss current evidence of someone's past vision.

☐ What is the difference between focus and vision?

Self-Reflection (use the journaling page or a dedicated notebook for your answers).

o What are some possible barriers that may keep you from focusing on your goals?

o Brainstorm ways around those barriers.

Assignment: Getting the Most out of this Principle

o Create your Vision/Dream Board (Refer to *Creating a Vision Board* in Appendix B.)

Success Principle 10 ~ Elevating Knowledge through Education

"The surest way to success in education, and in any other line for that matter, is to stick close to the common and familiar things that concern the greater part of the people the greater part of the time."

Knowledge is power. Each day, there are infinite opportunities to learn something new. As such, education is a never-ending process. Learn all that you can. Make your daily surroundings learning environments. For instance, you can turn your car into a "drive-time-university" by listening to audio versions of educational, motivational, or inspirational material. Keep in mind that listening is key to learning. It must be intentional and performed on a deeper level than merely hearing. Also, you can never learn while you're talking. Therefore, be discerning when deciding whether to speak or listen. There's a time for both. Choose wisely.

Reinforce learning by applying it outside of the walls where the learning takes place, e.g., in the classroom, a counseling session, church, or a seminar. Never be ashamed to ask questions if you don't know the answer. It can be surprising to learn how many others benefit when you ask a question that they were afraid to ask. Additionally, take notes to retain what you've learned.

Principle Ten instructs us to never form opinions based solely on "hand-me-down" knowledge, otherwise known as secondhand information. That is, knowledge derived only from hearing it from someone else. Perform due diligence by doing the research. This is especially important when our opinions have the potential to influence or make an impact on others. We must educate ourselves before passing on information. To be good stewards of knowledge, we must uphold the values of accuracy and integrity, ensuring that we are guided by well-informed sources and perspectives.

Discussion/Debate topics

☐ Review the Self-Reflection and Assignment from Success Principle 9.

☐ Why is effective communication critical to both teaching and learning?

☐ What is the difference between hearing and listening? Refer to *Active Listening Skills* in Appendix A.

Self-Reflection (use the journaling page or a dedicated notebook for your answers).

o What is your attitude towards your personal education? How did that attitude develop?

o Are there obstacles in the way of your attaining a good education? If so, what are they?

o Which of these obstacles can you control and how? Which can't you control and why?

Assignment: Getting the Most out of this Principle

o Research opposing philosophies on education. For example, the philosophies of W.E.B. Dubois and Booker T. Washington on education for Blacks in America in the late 19th and early 20th centuries. Write a 500–750 word double-spaced essay to compare and contrast the philosophies. (Refer to *Simple Steps to Developing an Effective Essay* in Appendix A.)

Success Principle 11 ~ Elevating Dignity through Work

"The actual sight of a first-class house that a man has built is ten times more potent than pages of discussion about a house that he ought to build, or perhaps could build."

Decent and in order, with dignity and integrity, is how we should approach every task we take on. Whether it's doing chores, running errands, or performing in the workplace. Whether a cashier, janitor, teacher, doctor, lawyer, or CEO—treat every aspect of any job as if it were the best job on earth. This is especially important if you want to move up, break into a new field, or get in the door of a promising company. Often, we must "crawl before we walk." It's important to let your work speak for itself. In turn, glowing recommendations will follow.

All work is honorable. Where would we be if everyone chose a field society deems "socially acceptable" or "elite", e.g., doctor, lawyer, entertainer, athlete? Nothing's wrong with these positions, but there would be no one to do the essential work that we all benefit from. Work such as construction, mechanics, waiting tables, manufacturing, and so on—these jobs make our lives comfortable. It's the seemingly unnoticeable that makes the noticeable possible. Thus, all work is dignified and respectable.

To have the best experience in any task you take on, take time to improve in areas where you're weak, and reward yourselves for areas where you're strong. When appropriate, dress for the job you want, not for the job you have. Don't carry negativity from the outside into your workplace, and don't let negativity coming from others determine your day.

Principle Eleven endorses the development of highly sought-after professionals and individuals. When you leave a job, make sure they'll miss you when you're gone, rather than be happy to see you go. You must strive to create a void that others yearn to fill. This is a testament to the dignity that you have infused into your work.

Discussion / Debate Topics

- ☐ Review the Self-Reflection and Assignment from Success Principle 10.
- ☐ Discuss assignment from Principle 10 on philosophies of education.
- ☐ How does one make any type of work honorable?
- ☐ Discuss interviewing techniques.
- ☐ What are the pros and cons of starting at the bottom versus beginning at the top?

Self-Reflection (use the journaling page or a dedicated notebook for your answers).

- o Complete the following sentences:

  - ➢ My dream job is . . .
  - ➢ Steps to achieving my dream job include . . .

Assignment: Getting the Most out of this Principle

- o Scan job sites and write down three jobs that appeal to you.
- o Develop a one-page resume and relate it to the job that appeals to you the most. (Find relevant and current examples online, in the library, in career books, etc.)

Success Principle 12 ~ Elevating Wealth through Financial Responsibility

"We must catch the spirit of modern progress and achievement or be shut out by those who have."

Don't confuse, "*the love of* money is the root of all evil" with "money is the root of all evil." The key words are—*the love of.* It's okay to have money. It's not okay to become so attached to it that we'll do anything to get it. It's also not wise to spend money impulsively, ending up with more month at the end of your money, than more money at the end of the month. The former usually results in having to borrow money to make it through, which can lead to financial turmoil. As financial expert Dave Ramsey put it, "You can't solve a problem while simultaneously creating one." By the way, that statement applies to more than just finances.

Whether we earn income through employment, entrepreneurship, or bank interest, if we want to realize financial growth, we must choose to use money wisely. As a rule of thumb, don't spend more money than you earn, and set a reasonable ratio to *save some, give some,* and *spend some.* When we avoid dept, and save, give, and spend wisely, money grows—partly through a logical process (refer to *Understanding How Money Grows* in Appendix B) and partly through karma—a principal law of cause and effect.

Principle Twelve advocates wealth creation. While understanding financial prosperity, you must pursue not just wealth, but also the ethical and responsible management of it. Through financial wisdom and ethical stewardship, we nurture prosperity with purpose. In the pursuit of wealth and financial stability, let us remember that it is through our financial choices that we can elevate not only our own lives and our family's lives, but also, we can elevate the lives of those who are less fortunate in and around our communities.

Discussion/Debate Topics

☐ Review the Self-Reflection and Assignment from Success Principle 11.

☐ Discuss how accumulating wealth may or may not lead to happiness and/or success.

☐ Who are examples of wealthy people whose lifestyles led to poverty and/or unhappiness?

☐ Who are examples of wealthy people who seem content? Why might that be?

Self-Reflection (use the journaling page or a dedicated notebook for your answers).

o Describe your attitude towards money.

o How do you believe that attitude developed?

Assignment: Getting the Most out of this Principle

o Pay attention to any financial or money related news on the television, Internet, or in print during the week. Write a 250–500 word double-spaced essay on what you learned, and whether you were surprised, disappointed, hopeful, excited, or unaffected by what you learned. (Refer to *Simple Steps to Developing an Effective Essay* in Appendix A.)

o Develop a monthly budget using $5,000.00 post-tax income as your monthly income. Include items such as rent, transportation, food, phone, etc. Also include the ratio for how much you plan to save, spend, and give. Consider who or what you will give to, and why.

o Prepare a presentation on an area of the program that has made an impact on you thus far. Make it adequate for delivering a three to five minute oral presentation. During the week, practice delivering it orally. (Refer to *Public Speaking Skills: How to Communicate with Confidence* in Appendix A.)

 Leading...

Quadrant Three Wrap Up ~ Leading by Example

Basic Truths of leading by Example:

➢ Acquiring knowledge is empowering.

➢ Never form opinions based on secondhand information.

➢ Great vision leads to lasting legacies.

➢ Approach every task with dignity.

➢ Living within our means makes life comfortable.

➢ The love of money can lead to misfortune.

Quadrant Three Activities:

1. Complete Goals Exercise. (Refer to *Creating S.M.A.R.T. Goals* in Appendix B.)

2. Pay attention to different leaders and their leadership styles (e.g., in the news, on television programs, in your surroundings). Notice the effectiveness or ineffectiveness of their styles. Be prepared to discuss.

10 Tips for developing effective leadership skills

✓ Take responsibility for where you are en route to where you want to be.

✓ Raise the bar within your means.

✓ Handle any task you take on with a leadership attitude.

✓ Become a role model by leading by example.

✓ Lead with the expectation of developing future leaders.

✓ Don't take leadership opportunities for granted.

✓ Lead with vision, dedication, and commitment.

✓ Take calculated risks.

✓ Treat others with the respect you expect in return.

✓ Continually make realistic, measurable goals.

Use the following page for self-reflections, notes, and to journal about your experience in Quadrant Three.

Notes/Journaling

_____

_____

_____

_____

_____

_____

_____

_____

_____

_____

_____

_____

_____

_____

_____

_____

_____

_____

_____

_____

_____

Rule of Thumb: When you leave a job, the goal is always to make them miss you when you're gone, rather than being happy to see you go.

PREPARE TO SOAR...

By the end of the fourth quadrant, you will become sound in awareness of how **gratitude, purpose, service,** and **excellence** play a critical role in your ability to *soar* in success. You will have mastered the last four of the sixteen success principles embodied in the concepts of **being, growing, leading,** and **soaring**.

QUADRANT FOUR ~ EXCELLING IN PERSEVERANCE

CULTIVATING AN ATTITUDE OF

"No man discouraged ever wins a victory."

Excelling in Perseverance is the by-product and the reward of the three preceding quadrants: *Building on a Foundation of Self-worth*, *Advancing Through Change*, and *Leading by Example*. *Excelling in Perseverance* is the collective demonstration of living each day steadfast in *gratitude*, *purpose*, *service*, and *excellence*.

As we venture into this final quadrant, Quadrant Four, we recognize that the legacy we craft is not solely for ourselves; it is a blueprint for those who come after us—a testament to Character Leadership, the enduring spirit of unity, and the exceptional perseverance that has brought us to this point in time.

 FOCUS EXERCISE:

Next to each letter in the word "Persevere" below, write a word that is related to perseverance.

P - _____

E - _____

R - _____

S - _____

E - _____

V - _____

E - _____

R - _____

E - _____

If you run out of ideas on your own refer to a thesaurus or dictionary for additional possibilities.

Success Principle 13 ~ The Power of Gratitude

"The years come but once, and swiftly pass on, bearing the ineffaceable record we place upon them. If we make them beautiful years, we must do it moment by moment as they glide before us."

With intention we can realize the countless blessings we receive each day. The greatest one happens to be the moment we wake up. It's there that we are presented with a brand new chance to get it right. There is a saying, *"No matter how dirty your past is, your future is spotless."* A bright future often comes down to a state of mind—choosing to allow the appreciation for what you do have, to overshadow any discontent for what you don't have.

If we're not careful, it's easy to get caught up in what's going wrong, leaving us mentally and emotionally exhausted. In turn, causing us to run on short fuses and quick tempers, losing sight of what's important—the sound mind that we uncovered in Success Principle One. For this reason, it's helpful to remember that it's scientifically impossible to experience feelings of gratitude and despair simultaneously. It's our choice that will make or break us. Choose to see each day as a gift, and another chance to get it right. Being aware of this alone is enough to create feelings of gratitude.

Within Principle Thirteen, we explore the art of infusing our lives with gratitude. Keep in mind, each day bears the mark that we leave on it when it's over. Let's take the time to be grateful daily so that we leave honorable marks. Let's choose to leave positive imprints that will last long after we're gone, creating meaningful legacies that future generations will benefit from.

Discussion/Debate Topics

☐ Review Quadrant Three Wrap Up Activities and Quadrant Four Focus Exercise.

☐ Review the Self-Reflection and Assignment from Success Principle 12.

☐ Why is it impossible to feel grateful and discouraged at the same time?

Self-Reflection (use the journaling page or a dedicated notebook for your answers).

o Imagine, by way of a miracle, you woke up one morning full of gratitude because suddenly your life was highly satisfying, stress-free, and extremely successful:

➢ What would that look like? (Include, where you are, what you have, who you're with, or not with, and what you are doing, or getting ready to do.)

➢ Besides you, who else would be able to tell that the miracle happened?

➢ What are the obstacles that stand in the way of making the miracle become a reality?

o Brainstorm strategies for removing the obstacles listed.

Assignment: Getting the Most out of this Principle

o Practice the power of being present by referring to the *Mindfulness Meditations* in Appendix C. Journal your experience.

o For at least one week, write down three to five things for which you are grateful each day. If you happen to have a difficult day, notice how you can't feel grateful and discouraged at the same time. Making this a habit builds inner strength in the same way that consistent exercise builds physical strength.

Success Principle 14 ~ The Power of Purpose

*"The thing to do when one feels sure that he has said or done the right thing .
. . is to stand still and keep quiet—if he is right, time will show it."*

Just about everything that inhabits or occurs on this planet has a purpose—people, animals, plants, mountains, rain, wind, and so on. Fortunately for us, people were born with the keen ability to figure out and enhance their purpose. Purpose is made more meaningful when it makes a direct or indirect connection to improving someone else's life.

Moreover, it is often revealed through the experiences of our past. It emerges out of our trials, mistakes, lessons learned, and achievements. We will know our purpose when we feel our passion—when we recognize a harmony in our *being* and in our *growing*. This is what drives purpose and turns our passion and compassion into action.

Principle Fourteen unveils a path to purpose. At times, purpose may be recognized without much thought. Other times, it will take careful analysis over our life. Whatever it takes to discover purpose, once it is known we must begin to live our lives accordingly, allowing our actions to reflect our purpose. Living with purpose, on purpose, is an incredible experience. As the saying goes, *if you don't stand for something, you'll fall for anything.* Therefore, with intentionality we stand for our purpose.

Discussion/Debate Topics

- ☐ Review the Self-Reflection and Assignment from Success Principle 13.

- ☐ Who is someone who lives out their purpose? What is it? How can you tell?

- ☐ Describe how purpose can have both direct and indirect impacts in the lives of others.

Self-Reflection (use the journaling page or a dedicated notebook for your answers).

- o Complete the following sentences:

  - ➤ The work I would do even if I didn't get paid to do it would be . . .

  - ➤ I am willing to do this work for free because . . .

Assignment: Getting the Most out of this Principle

- o Volunteer for at least one day at a facility of your choice that serves others (e.g., hospital, shelter, church, youth organization, school).

- o Write a 250–500 word double-spaced essay about your experience during and after your volunteer assignment. (Refer to *Simple Steps to Developing an Effective Essay* in Appendix A.)

Success Principle 15 ~ The Power of Service

"It is the quiet, unseen giving which never reaches the ear of the world that makes possible the existence of the best things of the world."

Service to others often emerges from the personal setbacks, mishaps, and valley experiences that we've made it through. Looking back on these moments of adversity allows us to empathize with the struggles of others, cultivating a genuine and profound sense of compassion. Sometimes it requires not forgetting where we come from. Or perhaps it's the remembrance of what those who came before us overcame to make life easier for us. We draw great strength from these reflections. This strength can be used to lift others up.

Humility is a requirement for serving the needs of others. It has been said, *"Humility is not thinking less of ourselves, it is thinking of ourselves less."* It is in this state of humility that we experience strength under control. There is no sentiment more humbling than, *"I cried because I had no shoes, until I met a man who had not feet."* It reminds us that our situation could always be worse and that maybe it has been. This is what commonly ignites a strong desire to serve.

Principle Fifteen guides the way to turn passion and compassion into action. There are endless opportunities to serve others. Ranging from simple random acts of kindness—a smile, a kind word, a hug, to providing more tangible needs—food, clothing, transportation, shelter. The act of service is not only a path to success, but a conduit for Character Leadership. Through service, we discover our shared humanity and that's what brings us together to elevate not only our character but also the character of the communities we serve.

Discussion/Debate Topics

☐ Review the Self-Reflection and Assignment from Success Principle 14.

☐ Are we our "Brother's Keeper?"

☐ What is the difference between purpose and service? How can they work together?

Self-Reflection (use the journaling page or a dedicated notebook for your answers).

o What thoughts drive your response when people who are less fortunate than you solicit you for money?

o How can you use your unique gifts and talents to help people in need? What population might you target?

Assignment: Getting the Most out of this Principle

o Write a 250-500 double-spaced essay about your volunteer assignment from Success Principle 14. (Refer to *Simple Steps to Developing an Effective Essay* in Appendix A.)

o Prepare a presentation on an area of the program that has made an impact on you thus far. Make it adequate for delivering a three to five minute oral presentation. During the week, practice delivering it orally. (Refer to *Public Speaking Skills: How to Communicate with Confidence* in Appendix A.)

Success Principle 16 ~ The Power of Excellence

"Excellence is to do a common thing in an uncommon way."

Excellence is the pinnacle of all the other principles. We are not born with excellence, but we are born with the ability to achieve excellence through hard work and dedication. Excellence is an internalized attitude. It's something we bring to life, not something we get from life. It's the way we look at the world, and what we do in the world that makes us excellent. For instance, when we choose to have an attitude of victory instead of defeat despite our circumstances, we are operating in excellence.

Most importantly, excellence is not perfection. The difference between the two is, being perfect is impossible, whereas striving for excellence is highly achievable. If we take little steps along the way, with excellence as the goal, we will embody it. In other words, put your best effort forth in all that you do. Even when something appears insignificant, approach it with excellence and excellence will start to spill over and permeate to other more significant areas in your life. Therefore, whether it is keeping your word, following through on a commitment, cleaning a room, prioritizing your day, ironing your clothes, or brushing your teeth; do it all with the intention of achieving excellence.

Principle Sixteen asserts that the benefits of striving for excellence far outweigh the satisfaction of mediocrity. An additional benefit is that once you commit to excellence, the habits you've developed will not leave even when missing the mark on occasion. In pursuit of excellence, we may revert to old behaviors that do not serve us well from time to time. But the good news is this, when you consistently strive to achieve excellence, it will begin to effortlessly find its way back to you.

Discussion/Debate Topics

- ☐ Review the Self-Reflection, and Assignment from Success Principle 15.

- ☐ What are the benefits of developing time management skills? (Refer to *Time Management Skills* in Appendix B.)

- ☐ Discuss findings from the *Leading by Example* Activity #2 in *Quadrant Three Wrap Up*.

Self-Reflection (use the journaling page or a dedicated notebook for your answers).

- o What are some ways that you can strive for excellence rather than perfection? How does that look different than striving for perfection?

Assignment: Getting the Most out of this Principle

- o Complete *Excellence Inventory Exercise*. (Refer to *Excellence Inventory* in Appendix C.)

- o Write a one-page, 250 word essay briefly describing how you might achieve an excellent outcome versus an average outcome in a situation that is important to you, e.g., work deadline, sports activity, class project, relationship issue. (Refer to *Simple Steps to Developing an Effective Essay* in Appendix A.)

 **Soaring...**

Quadrant Four Wrap Up ~ Excelling in Perseverance

Basic Truths of Excelling in Perseverance:

➢ **Perseverance requires grit and courage in difficult times.**

➢ **Humility is strength under control.**

➢ **It's impossible to experience gratitude and despair simultaneously.**

➢ **Operating in our purpose requires passion.**

➢ **Create the change you want to see through acts of service.**

➢ **Excellence over perfection is the goal.**

Quadrant Four Activities:

1. Describe five areas where you currently exercise excellence.

2. Imagine that you are living in your purpose. What does that look like? Use the journaling/notes page to capture your thoughts in writing.

3. Complete *S.W.O.R. Post Analysis* in Appendix B. (See instructions in *Quadrant One*)

10 Tips on How to Persevere in Excellence

✓ Expect excellence.

✓ Develop habits and cherish opportunities to create excellence.

✓ Never underestimate your potential to become excellent.

✓ Gratitude is developed by paying attention to the positive things in life.

✓ Excellence begins in our life the moment we decide that it will.

✓ Our past stories and our passion reveal our purpose.

✓ Use common sense to solve uncommon problems.

✓ Even during excellence, always be prepared for the inevitable storm.

✓ Through gratitude we endure the seemingly impossible and restore excellence.

✓ Live each day as if your legacy depends on it.

Final Exercise: Complete the following sentence:

The life I will lead while I'm here, and the legacy I will leave, will tell future generations that I . . .

Use the following page for self-reflections, notes, and to journal about your experience in Quadrant Four.

Notes/Journaling

Rule of Thumb: Strive to live in wholehearted balance. Don't spend all your time and energy in one area of your life (e.g., sports, a person, work) at the expense of neglecting other important areas (e.g., self-care, education, friends, and family).

Appendix A
Critical Thinking & Effective Verbal
& Written Communication

Thinking on A Deeper Level

It's easy to get lost in the crowd. Saying what they say, and thinking how they think. That may be fine for someone who is willing to settle for an unremarkable existence and a lackluster lifestyle. But for those who wish to leave an unforgettable blueprint in the world, merely existing in the crowd is not an option. That requires stepping out in an effort to lead. The following sections, *Critical Thinking: Six Steps to Become Proficient* and *Groupthink: What It Is and How to Avoid It,* are two thinking strategies that open up doors of influence in unimaginable ways, and in turn, help create that unforgettable blueprint, otherwise known as an extraordinary legacy.

Critical Thinking: Six Steps to Becoming Proficient

Critical thinking has been described as *thinking about thinking.* The Oxford English Dictionary describes it as an objective analysis and evaluation of an issue in order to form a judgement. Dozens of variations of this definition can be found. However, what most definitions have in common is that critical thinking is *the ability to think in an organized and rational fashion to draw associations between facts, opinions, and/or ideas, without bias.* In short, it's a well-thought out opinion or conclusion.

Thinking critically helps one to identify limitations in their own knowledge and shortfalls in their reasoning, and effectively bridge that gap. As a result, if asked to give a reason for an opinion, critical thinkers are prepared to provide concrete information to back up *why* they think *what* they think. Critical thinkers are set apart from those whose thoughts are based on what they hear from others without any knowledge to base their thoughts on. As such, critical thinking is antithetical to "group think", which happens when individuals in a group conform to the opinion of the group. This kind of thinking hinders creativity. See *Groupthink: What It Is and How to Avoid It* in Appendix A. The following are steps necessary to become a critical thinker.

Six Key Steps to Critical Thinking:

1. **Identify an issue:** It's important here to be as specific and concise as possible.
   Example: *"According to popular belief, longer school days in kindergarten lead to improved academic performance in high school."*

2. **Gather sources:** Be sure to include sources that offer different angles, ideas, and perspectives. Make sure they are relevant, reliable, and credible sources. If the issue concerns Americans, don't gather sources from Africa. Have at least four sources for each side of the issue. For reliability and credibility, peer-reviewed articles are excellent. Make sure that your sample size is adequate.

3. **Consider context:** Focusing on an issue without context is futile. Be sure to consider all significant context, i.e., period in history, surroundings, conditions. All are vitally important to the issue at hand.

4. **Identify biases/assumptions:** Identify your source's biases and your own biases. As much as possible, gather sources that are objective, neutral, and balanced. This won't always be easy. Regarding your biases, try to keep an open mind. Don't be so attached to your view that there is no room to process all thought.

5. **Prioritize level of importance:** Organize sources by the order of significance to the issue at hand. This will especially come in handy when it's time to articulate your conclusion.

6. **Formulate a conclusion:** Considering all the new information you have, answer the following questions: What are the strengths and weaknesses of the arguments for and against the issue? Which side is more supported by the evidence? Has your initial thought changed or stayed the same? Why or why not?

On a final note, common traits among the savviest critical thinkers are their willingness to keep learning, their open-mindedness, and their readiness to change as the evidence changes. The sharpest critical thinkers are willing to admit that as smart as they may appear, there is so much they don't know. Which gives credence to Aristotle's quote, "The more you know, the more you realize you don't know." This is a common belief held by the most astute critical thinkers.

Groupthink: What It Is and how to Avoid It

Groupthink is a psychological concept that involves conforming to a group's norms, beliefs, and opinions at the expense of voicing one's individual point of view. This often results from not wanting to disrupt the cohesiveness of a group, or it may result from an effort to fit in. It can also be the result of the inability or unwillingness to think for oneself.

The biggest downside to groupthink is that it stifles creativity. It can also cause regret within the person who keeps quiet. It may even cause resentment that eventually damages the so-called cohesiveness of the group. This is especially true when a group decision ends up in failure.

An example of groupthink: Suppose you and five friends decide to get together at the end of the week to plan a vacation. You recently read about a Caribbean vacation resort on a secluded beach. You can't wait to tell your friends all about it. All week you pictured the six of you relaxing on the beautiful white sand, clearwater beaches, away from all the hustle and bustle of the city life where you currently live and work.

Once you are all together, you open your mouth to speak, and before you can get the first word out, one friend enthusiastically shares a brochure for a trip to New York. The trip includes Broadway shows, shopping, dining, and city tours. Another friend expresses how exciting that sounds. Another chimes in and says she's always wanted to shop on 5th Avenue and dine in Manhattan. The last two friends share how they have always wanted to visit Times Square.

While you sit quietly disappointed, they turn to you and ask for your opinion. Do you say, "I was thinking about a relaxing Caribbean vacation"? Or do you go along to get along? The latter is an example of groupthink. It may be harmless to go along to get along when it comes to being with friends on vacation. But what about when you are involved in making a life-changing decision. Or even a less critical decision that may have long-term effects. For instance, deciding who will lead a team or how to prioritize activities of an important project. Below are tips to help circumvent the limits that groupthink creates.

Tips for Avoiding Groupthink:

As a group:

1. Have a brainstorming session where no idea is off the table.

2. Encourage "out of the box" thinking.

3. Leave "this is how we've always done it" thinking out of the room.

4. Have a reflection period to process ideas individually away from the group.

5. Return from the reflection period with reasons to back up individual ideas.

As an individual:

1. Believe in your ideas and the value they bring.

2. Have a sincere, thought-out position to back up your ideas.

3. Pick your battles carefully. Ask yourself if dissent is worth the energy.

4. Practice bringing your ideas to the table with someone you trust.

5. Have the courage to listen carefully to possible rejection and respond tactfully.

How to Conduct an Organized Mini Debate

An organized debate is a structured discussion around a particular issue. There are two teams representing opposing views. One team will be for the issue, representing the affirmative point of view. The other team will be against the issue, representing the opposing point of view.

Other critical components of an organized debate include debate preparation; oral presentation of each team's position on the issue; rebuttal period; and closing statements. These are explained further in the instructions. To hone debating skills, refer to *Communicating with Confidence; Active Listening Skills; Critical Thinking: Six Steps to Becoming Proficient;* and *Groupthink: What It Is and How to Avoid It* in Appendix A, and *Self-fulfilling Prophecy and the Law of Suggestion* in Appendix C.

Participants will learn how to:

- ✓ Engage in critical thinking
- ✓ Support, clarify, and defend their position
- ✓ Research and organize source material
- ✓ Draw conclusions from source material
- ✓ Work well alone and within a team
- ✓ Deliver polished presentations
- ✓ Disagree with tact and respect
- ✓ Exercise self-control
- ✓ Communicate effectively
- ✓ Listen attentively
- ✓ Maintain focus

Needs for the debate

1. Participants: Judge(s), team participants (four presenters total, two on each team), timekeeper

2. Audience (This may be the remainder of the group once the team members and judge(s) are selected)

3. Evaluation/Score Sheet (provided in instructions)

4. Writing instruments (pens or pencils)

5. 3x5 Index cards

6. Note paper

Preparing for the debate (1 hour)

- ☐ Establish rules, such as, be courteous; be respectful; don't interrupt; no cursing; don't use harsh tones or derogatory and demeaning language. (5 minutes)

- ☐ Choose an issue to debate. There are various methods to determine this, including brainstorming issues, then, either vote, conduct a random drawing, or have the facilitator choose an issue. (10 minutes)

- ☐ Decide who will be on teams, which team will be for the issue (the affirmative position), and which will be against (the opposing position); and who will judge. There are various methods to determine this as well, (e.g., volunteer, vote, have the facilitator choose, draw names, coin flip). The affirmative position goes first. (2–1/2 minutes)

- ☐ Within each team, decide which member will present first, and which one will give the closing statement. See methods above for ideas on how to decide. (2–1/2 minutes)

- ☐ For the opening and closing statements, all presenters will research the issue seeking to find two to three facts, two to three expert opinions, and two to three analogies or examples. (25 minutes) Use the note paper to take notes based on your findings.

- ☐ Each presenter will create an outline for a strong case based on the research, making sure to develop at least three, and no more than four points to present their position. Ensure that these points are different from their partner's points and are succinct and will fit into the allotted time. (15 minutes) Use the index cards for the outline.

Note: Include philosophical, historical, economic, statistical, and/or current event information in the three to four points. Search newspapers, expert blogs, journals, peer-reviewed articles, literature reviews, etc.

Presenting Positions During the Debate (6–10 minutes)

- ☐ With the affirmative team going first, each team orally presents their position on the issue using the points developed from their research. (3–5 minutes each)

  Notes: While each team presents, the other team listens intently and takes notes. These notes will be used to formulate crossfire questions, and to strengthen their team's position, while attempting to weaken the other team's position.

Preparation for Rebuttal Question and Answers (10 minutes)

- ☐ After opening statements, debate will pause to allow each team to develop three to five questions based on their notes, to pose during the rebuttal period coming next. (5 minutes)

- ☐ Participants will also try to think of the rebuttal questions the opponents might ask, so that they may mentally prepare to answer accordingly. (5 minutes)

  Note: Check to ensure that partners have different questions.

Rebuttal Period (10–14 minutes)

☐ Once the teams reconvene after the rebuttal preparation period, the question and answer session will begin, starting with the team that presented first asking their three to five questions. (5–7 minutes)

☐ The team which presented second will then ask their three to five questions. (5-7 minutes)

Notes:

o Rebuttal questions and answers should be concise and to the point, courteous and respectful.

o Questions and responses should not be sarcastic, rude, demeaning, or insulting.

o One team member may ask the questions while the other listens and takes notes.

Preparation for Closing Statements (10 minutes)

☐ Teams will pause after rebuttal period to develop remarks around their team's strengths and the other team's weaknesses. (10 minutes)

Note: Take the strongest, most persuasive points and counter arguments to develop an outline.

Closing Statements (6–10 minutes)

☐ Once teams reconvene after the preparation for the closing statements, the first team to present will present their closing statement, followed by the second team. (3–5 minutes each)

Note: Be sure to be succinct and concise so that the closing statement fits within the allotted time.

Final Notes: It makes for a particularly interesting and challenging debate when people who are against an issue have to argue in favor of it, and vice versa.

The above instructions are recommendations and may be modified to fit different situations.

Order of Debate Sheet   **Approximate Time:** 1 hour 45 minutes to 2 hours

Order of Debate	Participants	Participants	Time Limit
Debate preparation	Entire Group	Entire Group	1 hour
Present issue and team's position (Opening statement)	Affirmative Team	Speaker #1	3–5 Minutes
Present issue and team's position (Opening statement)	Opposing Team	Speaker #1	3–5 Minutes
Pause to prepare for rebuttal	All Team Participants	All Team Participants	10 Minutes
Rebuttal period	From Affirmative Team	To Opposing Team	5–7 Minutes
Rebuttal period	From Opposing Team	To Affirmative Team	5–7 Minutes
Preparation for closing statements	All Team Participants	All Team Participants	10 Minutes
Closing statement	From Affirmative Team	Speaker #2	3–5 Minutes
Closing statement	From Opposing Team	Speaker #2	3–5 Minutes

Debate Evaluation/Score Sheet

To rate participants, select from 1 through 5 below, with 1 being poor and 5 being excellent. Add the selected numbers together. Add totals of both team partners together to get the winning team.

Participant Name: Debate Topic:	Date:		Team: A = Affirmative O = Opposing
Judging Criteria	Debate Issue:		Date:
On a scale of 1 to 5 with 1 being poor, and 5 being excellent, rate the following:	Opening	Rebuttal	Closing
Research material was organized	1 2 3 4 5	1 2 3 4 5 N/A	1 2 3 4 5 N/A
Time limits were adhered to	1 2 3 4 5	1 2 3 4 5	1 2 3 4 5
Adequate balance of facts, expert opinions, analogies and/or examples	1 2 3 4 5	1 2 3 4 5	1 2 3 4 5
Outline of no more than three to four points for opening/closing	1 2 3 4 5	N/A	1 2 3 4 5
Used proper grammar, vocabulary, avoided slang	1 2 3 4 5	1 2 3 4 5	1 2 3 4 5
Used philosophical, historical, social, economic, statistical, and/or current event information	1 2 3 4 5	1 2 3 4 5	1 2 3 4 5
Made connections between the issue and social, economic, and/or political matters or trends	1 2 3 4 5	1 2 3 4 5	1 2 3 4 5
Presented clearly and logically, with a demonstrated understanding of the issue	1 2 3 4 5	1 2 3 4 5	1 2 3 4 5
Utilized a variety of resources (e.g., newspapers, blogs, journals, books)	1 2 3 4 5	1 2 3 4 5	1 2 3 4 5
Presented different information than partner(s)	N/A	1 2 3 4 5	1 2 3 4 5 N/A
Questions and answers were relevant and logical	N/A	1 2 3 4 5	N/A
Stayed concise and to the point, keeping redundancy to a minimum	1 2 3 4 5	1 2 3 4 5	1 2 3 4 5
Did not interrupt	1 2 3 4 5	1 2 3 4 5	1 2 3 4 5
Stayed respectful	1 2 3 4 5	1 2 3 4 5	1 2 3 4 5
Made eye-contact, and demonstrated poise and confidence	1 2 3 4 5	1 2 3 4 5	1 2 3 4 5
Demonstrated persuasive oral-speaking skills	1 2 3 4 5	1 2 3 4 5	1 2 3 4 5

Active Listening Skills

10 Critical listening skills that lead from "blah-blah-blah," to enriched conversations

Remember, if you want to be heard, and more importantly, understood, you have to communicate in a way that can be received. What's more, you can only learn when you're listening, not when you're talking. Active listening requires the listener to listen intentionally, while demonstrating interest and respect.

As you hone listening skills, your conversations become richer and more meaningful. You may even convert rivals into supporters as they are more willing to listen to you in turn. The following skills take practice and may require breaking long-standing habits.

Active Listening Skills:

1. Start with a genuinely curious demeanor. Purposely conjure it up if you must.

2. Give your undivided attention; put aside all distracting thoughts; and while the other person is speaking, don't mentally prepare for your "great" comeback.

3. Do everything in your power to avoid interrupting.

4. Don't allow personal filters (assumptions; judgements; cultural, religious, and/or political beliefs) to cloud your judgement or distract you from the conversation at hand.

5. Be aware that non-verbal communication speaks loudly.

6. Indicate that you are listening with your gestures (e.g., nod, smile, and use facial expressions as appropriate).

7. Indicate that you are listening with your body language, (e.g., make sure your posture is open and inviting, as opposed to closed and guarded).

8. Occasionally make verbal cues for the speaker to continue, by using words such as "yes," and/or "uh-huh."

9. Make eye to eye contact. It is okay to look away occasionally, but the bulk of the time should be spent making eye contact.

10. When you are confused, ask, "What do you mean when you say . . .?" Or, reflect back to them with what you think they meant, by saying, "Sounds like you are saying . . . ." Then allow for confirmation or clarification.

In the final analysis, keep in mind that active listening requires intention, interest, and respect. It requires the same consideration that the listener would expect when they are speaking. This kind of listening reaps great rewards for everyone involved.

Mastering the Art of Using I–Statements

It's important to keep in mind that there is a huge difference between personal opinions and facts. When we make statements during an argument that begin with, "You are . . ." or "You never . . ." not only do these statements sound like facts—when they may actually be opinions—but they imply that these behaviors describe the whole person, and the behaviors will always be there.

What's more, when we experience negative feelings due to someone else's actions, we tend to make assumptions, give ultimatums, criticize, demand, threaten, and even attack or assassinate their character. Clearly, these behaviors will not lead to a positive outcome. More likely, they will lead to anger, defensiveness, or fear. What's worse, unintended, irreversible emotional damage may ensue, and arise when we least expect it to. Remember, negativity breeds more negativity, just as positivity breeds more positivity.

The opposite of an I-Statement is a You-Statement. Following are common examples of You-statements:

Destructive Action:	Example:
o Analyzing	"It's because you always hang out with them."
o Doubting	"I can never believe anything you say."
o Blaming/Accusing	"If it weren't for you, I'd be much further along."
o Sarcasm	"You know everything."
o Threatening	"If you don't . . . I will . . ."
o Criticizing	"You never appreciate anything I do."
o Labeling	"You're crazy!"
o Demanding	"You better listen to me!"
o Demeaning	"You can't compete with them."
o Moralizing/Comparing	"You should be more like the others."

When we are experiencing negative feelings, it's common for us to blame others for making us feel the way we do. It's also common to make over-generalizations when we communicate with them about our feelings (e.g., "You always . . ." "Every time you come around . . ."). However, accepting responsibility for our feelings is a much more effective way for us to communicate, and to solve problems.

The best way to accept responsibility for our feelings is by using I-Statements. When we use I-Statements accurately it can be a very effective technique. There are three main parts to an I-Statement. An I-Statement should explain *how we feel*; *when we feel that way*; and, *why we feel that way*. For example, "I **feel** frustrated **when** you don't finish your work, **because** it makes more work for me."

There are major personal and relational benefits that I-Statements promote. They include creating personal power to influence change, instead of merely placing blame and leaving it there; they allow us to express feelings and emotions without hostility; and they minimize offensive or retaliatory behavior.

A Few I-Statement Precautions

1. I-Statements are an appeal for help, both parties must be willing to resolve the problem.

2. It is important that each person feels listened to when they speak and respond.

3. If either person is unwilling to listen, this technique will not work.

The presence or absence of these precautions, will determine whether or not professional help is warranted, or if it may be necessary to distance yourself from the relationship.

Simple Steps to Develop an Effective Essay

Writing is a very powerful form of communication. This is especially true because, unlike speaking, writing doesn't vanish once the words are out. If you want to impress upon someone an idea that will linger, there's no better way to achieve that than to send it in writing. Following are simple steps to writing an effective essay.

Step One: Develop the Outline

On the top of the page, write the name of your topic.

1. Down the left-hand side of the page, write numbers 1, 2, and 3, and write down the three main ideas/points that you plan to make in your essay.

   ➤ To inform: establish three categories regarding your topic that you want to inform your readers about and list them next to each number.

   ➤ To persuade: develop three strong arguments regarding what you are trying to get your readers to do or think about.

   ➤ To explain: break the topic down into steps that the reader is to follow. Group the steps into three categories, beginning, middle, and end.

2. Under each main idea/point, write a, b, and c, and next to each letter write the information, including facts, statistics, etc. that will support the main idea/point.

Step Two: Develop a Thesis Statement

The thesis statement tells the reader what the essay topic will be about. You will want to refer to your outline to see what the main ideas and supporting ideas say about your topic.

Thesis statements have two parts. The first part deals with the topic, for example:

➤ Freedom of Speech in America

➤ How to Create an Extraordinary Legacy

The second part of the thesis statement discusses the main idea/point of the essay:

➤ Freedom of speech in America is not free

➤ Creating your extraordinary legacy takes commitment and diligence

Upon completing the outline and thesis statement you will be prepared to begin the body of the essay, where you will describe, persuade, argue, and/or explain your topic.

Each of your main ideas in the outline will serve to create the body paragraphs of your essay. In the case of these instructions, you will have three body paragraphs.

Step Three: Develop Body Paragraphs

➢ Write your main ideas/points in a sentence. If your main idea is, "Freedom of Speech in America is not Free" you might write, "Freedom of speech in America is not free because those with the most money have the loudest voices."

➢ Prepare three supporting points for the main idea, leaving four to five lines between each point to develop them further in the next step.

➢ Using the four to five lines of empty space that you reserved earlier, develop each point, elaborating through explaining, discussing, and/or describing your point.

Step Four: Develop Supporting Points

➢ Supporting points should include evidence (e.g., facts, statistics, and expert opinion). For instance, "Freedom of speech belongs to those with money because research indicates people are influenced more by those with wealth, than those with little money." Be prepared to cite the sources of the research.

After each of the body paragraphs have been fleshed out for each main point, it will be time to write the introduction and conclusion of your essay.

Step Five: Develop the Introduction

In addition to giving a focal point to the essay, it is essential that the introduction grabs the reader's attention. Effective ways of doing this are as follows:

➢ A shocking statement: Make sure that it is true, and that it can be verified. After the statement, write down one or two sentences with your own point of view, or other information that helps to support the statement.

➢ An anecdote: An illustrative short story that is to the point and relevant to the topic.

➢ Two to three brief and relevant exchanges/dialogues between two or three people. Be sure to elaborate with your own ideas.

➢ Summarize: About three sentences, from general to specific, that lead to the thesis.

Step Six: Conclusion

You want to be sure to bring closure to your content with a final viewpoint on the topic. A strong conclusion will begin with, "In conclusion . . .," followed by an anecdote or your own thoughts in three or four strong sentences that reiterate the main points without repeating them verbatim.

Tips for Strengthening Your Essay

- ➢ Always use spell/grammar check.

- ➢ Ask trusted others to review/proofread your essay.

- ➢ Consider putting one of the strongest paragraphs at the beginning of the essay, and another of the strongest paragraphs at the end, making certain that the order makes sense.

- ➢ Ensure that the formatting is correct as directed by your instructor or the instructions.

- ➢ Review your writing.

- ➢ Ensure that the sentences and paragraphs have smooth transitions.

- ➢ Words such as, "thus" or "nonetheless," may assist in making smooth transitions from sentence to sentence.

- ➢ References to a word or phrase in the previous paragraph may assist in making smooth transitions from paragraph to paragraph.

- ➢ Ensure that every sentence makes logical sense.

- ➢ Walk away from it for a while and come back with a fresh pair of eyes.

Writing is a very powerful form of communication. This is especially true because, unlike speaking, writing doesn't vanish once the words are out. If you want to impress upon someone an idea that will linger, there's no better way to achieve that than to send it in writing. Following are simple steps to writing an effective essay.

Public Speaking Skills: Communicating with Confidence

According to a Forbes Magazine article, "*Five Reasons Why the Fear of Public Speaking is Great for You*" for the average person, public speaking is the number one fear, followed by death at number two. The article goes on to state, "That means to the average person if you have to be at a funeral, you would rather be in the casket than doing the eulogy."

It's normal, natural, and even healthy to feel some nervousness before speaking to an audience. Even the most experienced and polished speakers experience butterflies. The key is to make the butterflies fly in formation. Once you grasp the skill of public speaking, you'll be able to congratulate yourself for accomplishing a task that most people will only dream about.

First, let's look at some of the benefits of public speaking.

Developing public speaking skills improves your ability to:

- ➢ Speak clearly and confidently before an audience.
- ➢ Train others to do a job that you have experience in.
- ➢ Lead meetings effectively.
- ➢ Influence or persuade others to do something that you believe is important.
- ➢ Land many opportunities (e.g., jobs, college admittance, auditions).

With preparation and practice, anyone can speak in public exceptionally well. Without these two components you are bound to be abnormally nervous, not feel in control, appear doubtful of your content, and seem apprehensive in your delivery. As a result, you and your audience will suffer.

The following points regarding preparation and practice will help you avoid having any of these adverse experiences. They are made up of the acronym, S.P.E.A.K., Structure, Practice, Engage, Acknowledge, Keep at it.

Structure

- ➢ Structure what you want to say in an outline format.
- ➢ It's best to organize your outline with a strong opening statement of three to four points, which make up the body of your speech, and an equally strong closing statement.
- ➢ You will want to especially memorize the opening and closing statements.
- ➢ The body of your speech can be written word for word when you are preparing, but should be in outline form on index cards when you deliver the speech.
- ➢ Your first statement should be an attention grabber (e.g., a statistic, a compelling story, a recent headline, or a fact that your audience relates to).

Practice

➤ Once you have prepared what you want to say, practice, practice, practice, until what you want to say begins to flow naturally. When it's time to speak to your audience you want it to sound conversational, and not rehearsed.

➤ Practice using your outline, or index cards with just enough words to trigger your memory. You never want to read word for word looking down at your notes.

➤ Speak at a pace that is easy for the audience to follow, not too fast, and not too slow.

➤ Practice pausing for a few seconds after you have made an important point so that the audience can digest and process what you have just said. Pauses also help you to gather your thoughts so that you sound natural and confident.

➤ Seek opportunities to speak in front of others (e.g., rotary clubs, fraternal organizations, family, and friends).

➤ Practice breathing exercises that will help to calm butterflies, (or at least get them to fly in formation). Nervousness is a natural part of public speaking that most speakers have.

➤ Repeating tongue-twisters helps improve pronunciation and articulation. They also help strengthen necessary muscles for speech through practicing the correct placement of the tongue, lips, and teeth. For example, no need to light a nightlight on a light night like tonight. Or, she sells seashells by the seashore.

➤ Speaking Circles® and Toastmasters are two organizations that help individuals develop public speaking skills. These organizations help aspiring speakers and leaders to eliminate unnecessary filler words; improve voice inflection; and master speaking on the spot, otherwise known as extemporaneous speaking. This kind of support can be invaluable.

Engage

➤ Whenever possible, arrive early so that you may walk around the room and engage with some of the audience members before it is time for you to speak. This helps the audience to warm up to you, and it helps you to feel less nervous once you begin speaking.

➤ Once you begin to speak, engage the audience by making eye contact all around the room. Be careful not to stare, and not to look at only one or two audience members. It may make them uncomfortable and make the rest of the room feel ignored.

➤ Find friendly faces that will help you feel supported as you speak. Keep your eye on them for three to five seconds, or until you finish a sentence, before going on to someone else.

➤ To make your audience feel engaged, at the start of your speech, ask a leading question, or ask for a show of hands.

Acknowledge

➢ Keep in mind that, while there may be a small percentage of naysayers in every audience, most of the audience will want you to succeed. In other words, they are there to listen, learn, and be supportive of you.

➢ What you have to say is for the benefit of the audience. Concentrate on them, and not on yourself, especially if you are thinking about not performing well.

➢ Remember that what you have to say is important, and people need to hear it.

➢ If you believe you will do well, you will. And if you believe you will do badly, most likely, you will. Thus, tell yourself often just how well you are going to do.

➢ Visualize yourself speaking in front of an audience and imagine them giving you an overwhelmingly positive response. This goes a long way towards making it actually happen.

Keep at it

➢ When the speech is over, breathe a sigh of relief. However, you're not done. Whenever possible, to record your speech so that you can watch it later.

➢ Watch for your body language, facial expressions, gestures, and filler words (e.g., "you know", "ah", "um", "like"). This will help you to improve in areas where you feel weak and maintain in areas where you believe you do well.

➢ Before you know it, you will be a polished speaker, ready to take advantage of all the aforementioned benefits of public speaking.

Netiquette: Effective Online Communication

In this era of modern technology and electronic communication, your reputation and your character are on the line every time you hit the send button. Opportunities may easily fall by the wayside because employers, professional associates, and others who may have the ability to open doors, have access to more information about you than ever before. Below is a list intended to give you a heads-up on how to keep your online presence pristine, your reputation classy, and your character in good standing.

Abbreviations. For business and academic writing (unless instructed otherwise), don't use abbreviations as you might with personal text-messaging or e-mail. For example, BTW (by the way) or LOL (laugh out loud). When appropriate to use abbreviations, first spell the word out and put the abbreviation that you plan to use in the document in parenthesis. For example, Department of Energy (DOE). After that, you may use DOE for all other references to the Department of Energy.

All Capital Letters. Writing an entire message using CAPITAL letters comes across as SHOUTING. It may cause a reaction that you don't intend, and lead to a response you don't like.

Chain Letters. Never forward these types of emails. They can represent superstitions, and more often than some may think, recipients are annoyed when they receive them.

Emojis/Emoticons. Just as with abbreviations, for business and academic writing, do not use emojis or emoticons, such as a smile made up of symbols, for example, :). Save these for friends and family members.

Flaming. Flaming is a hostile interaction between Internet users. This is **never** a good idea. It's best to sleep on whatever the issue is and handle it verbally when you're calm. Along the same lines, it is never a good idea to intentionally belittle, embarrass, or disrespect another person online. Keep negative business to yourself and you'll have no regrets later.

Fonts, Structure, and Layout. Some fonts are difficult to read, especially in script, or a size 10 or smaller. When possible, use a size 12 font, and a style that's easy to read, (e.g., Times New Roman, Arial, or Calibri). It is also much easier, and pleasant, to read short sentences with one line between paragraphs. You might even use bullets when making four or more specific points.

Grammar. Always practice using correct grammar, even when communicating with friends. This way, you will develop good habits that will endure when writing to business or academic associates.

Group Texting/Chats. Individuals are often involved in at least one group, e.g., work group, family, social, community. When posting or responding be sure that messages are relevant to everyone. Don't go off on a tangent that not everyone is interested in. For example, you start off asking questions about an upcoming meeting, and two people in the group begin discussing what they are having for dinner. Try to keep individual responses to no more than three brief comments in a row so that other's comments are not lost in multiple comments made by one person.

High Priority Important Urgent. Use these send options, and/or words, sparingly. And never indicate that an email is high priority, important, or urgent if it isn't.

Long Messages. Unless you are on Twitter, aka X, which only allows a limited number of characters, it is up to you to keep your messages concise and to the point. Leave out filler words and fluff, otherwise known as unnecessary words. A reader may delete your message rather than get bogged down in it. This can be especially true when they are busy. Hence, they may end up missing out on some very important information that you wanted them to see.

Message Threads. A thread is what occurs each time a recipient replies to one original message. Threads can become extremely long. In order not to get lost in the thread or end up printing pages and pages when you only want a page, after a few replies to an email, consider starting a fresh email with a new subject line. In some instances, you may need the long thread. Use wise judgement.

Personal/Confidential Information. Keep personal business personal. Putting confidential information online can lead to numerous backlashes, i.e., hurt feelings, embarrassment for yourself and/or others, termination from a job. If you don't want the world to know, don't send it electronically. There is a reason it's called the World Wide Web.

Proofreading. Whether you are texting, emailing, sending a tweet, or a Facebook message, always read your message before you hit the send button. For longer messages, if you do not have spell/grammar check in the application that you are sending it in, cut and paste to a Word document, and do the spell/grammar check there. Paste it back into the original application and then send.

Replying to All. Unless everyone needs to see your response to an email, using this option can be quite annoying. Use the singular reply option instead, so that only the original sender gets your response.

Respond in a Timely Manner. Everyone's busy in this fast-paced world we live in. It's great to have electronic messages to communicate these days because we can do so at our leisure instead of the moment someone reaches out. However, be considerate when someone sends an electronic message to you by returning at least a brief acknowledgement that you received it. If it requires a response and you're short on time, politely let them know that you'll respond with more information when time permits. For friends and family, an appropriate emoticon or GIF image will do. But just don't leave people hanging, wondering if you even received the message.

Sending Messages to Large Groups of People. Always protect the addresses of your recipients. Unless you have prior permission from each recipient, do not place the addresses where others can see them. Rather, put all the addresses in the BCC (blind copy) field, and only have your address showing on the To line.

Subject Line. Always make sure that there is content in the subject line before hitting the send button. It should be clear and concise so that the recipient can get a good idea of what the mail is about.

Using the Internet in School or Place of Business. More likely than not, the organization where the computer is housed legally owns all internal and external information that is sent on their computers. Keep in mind that everything you do can end up in the dean's, the principal's, human resources, or even the CEO's office, and result in your embarrassment, suspension, expulsion, or termination.

Viruses Camouflaged as a Link. Even when an e-mail with an HTML link comes from a trusted source, think twice before opening it and/or forwarding it. When it is highly suspect, for example, an email with nothing but a link in the body of the email, move it to a spam folder. You may also contact the sender to find out if they really sent the link to you, and if they know whether or not it is safe to open.

Wording and Sentence Structure. Since writing does not come with the same effects that face-to-face communication does, (e.g., hand gestures, facial expressions, and vocal intonation) be mindful of the words you chose, your punctuation (especially exclamation points), and your sentence structure.

One Final Note: Leave private moments private. Be present in your life without having the urge to send every picture, thought, or emotion you have every time you snap it, think it, or feel it. Don't rob yourself and those in your presence of precious moments. Be careful not to overwhelm others with your life. Also, use your judgement on what others may or may not want to see. You might be surprised at just how many people are not interested in seeing wounds, scars, IV feeds, blood, insects, dead animals, etc. Lastly, careful on the boasting and save the venting for your best friend.

Three Rules of Thumb:

- ✓ Everything in moderation.
- ✓ Do unto others as you would have them do unto you.
- ✓ Use social media wisely so that it doesn't use you.

APPENDIX B
WORK/LIFE MANAGEMENT

Four-Week Personal Fitness Plan

This four-week plan is meant to be a simple and doable guide. Consult with your medical practitioner for help in designing a fitness plan that is best for you, especially if you have an injury, medical condition, or are currently under a doctor's care.

The purpose of the plan is to create concrete steps toward:

- ✓ Raising the level of awareness of the importance of physical health.
- ✓ Developing a new plan or maintaining a plan that is already in place.
- ✓ Starting or maintaining a journey toward a physically healthier lifestyle.

Tips for making an effective plan:

- ☐ Think of this plan as an investment in YOU, and a path to creating a lifestyle.
- ☐ Fitness goals should be realistic, and not overwhelming.
- ☐ Focus on the progress that is being made, no matter how small.
- ☐ Progress should be measured in terms of new healthy habits.
- ☐ Reward consistency. For example, drinking 8 to 10 glasses of water 5 days in a row.
- ☐ Stay aware of stressors that may lead to unhealthy habits.
- ☐ Be sure to include healthy fitness habits you enjoy, such as walking, swimming, dancing, etc.

Getting started:

In your own words, write down three to five realistic actions you will take within a four-week period to create or maintain healthier habits. For example:

- ☐ I will drink 8 to 10, 8-ounce glasses of water daily.
- ☐ I will exercise at least 30 minutes per day, at least 4 days per week.
- ☐ I will increase the amount of fruits and vegetables I eat daily.
- ☐ I will decrease the amount of fried and sugary foods I eat.
- ☐ I will be sure to get a balanced amount of rest and relaxation each day.

1. _____

2. _____

3. _____

4. _____

5. _____

After your list is complete, and before you start your plan, make a note of how you feel emotionally most days out of a normal week, e.g., tired, vibrant, unhappy, happy, irritated, motivated, or unmotivated.

At the end of each of the four weeks, note how you feel emotionally most days out of each week, e.g., tired, vibrant, unhappy, happy, irritated, motivated, or unmotivated.
Use the sheet on the next page to record your accomplishments each day.

Finally, tailor the plan to meet your unique abilities. Remember, if you fall short or totally miss the mark on occasion, don't beat yourself up, just get up, and get back on track. For example, on the sample plan less than eight glasses of water are listed on some days. Each new day presents a brand new chance to get it right.

Note: No content in this book should ever be used as a substitute for direct medical advice from your doctor or other qualified clinician.

Four-Week Personal Fitness Plan

Name: _____ Start Day and Date:_____

Monday	Tuesday	Wednesday	Thursday	Friday	Saturday	Sunday
Sample Week Walked 2 miles. Drank 8 glasses of water. Decided not to eat any fried foods this week.	Walked 3 miles. Drank 5 glasses of water. No fried food.	Walked/Ran 3 miles. Drank 6 glasses of water. No fried food.	Worked out at the gym for 30 minutes. Drank 8 glasses of water. No fried or sugary foods.	Worked out at the gym for 30 minutes. Drank 7 glasses of water. Ate 5 servings of vegetables/ fruits.	Went out dancing. Drank 8 glasses of water. Ate 5 servings of vegetables/ fruits.	Rest and relaxation day. Drank 8 glasses of water. Ate 5 servings of vegetables/ fruits.
Week One						
Week Two						
Week Three						
Week Four						

Core Values Exercise

Though we may not always be conscious of what they are, we all have values. When we are aware of our values, we are more likely to live by them, stand on them, and make choices that honor them. Follow the directions below to hone in on the values which are most important to you.

Directions:

Use the blank spaces in the table below to list as many of your core values as you can think of. You may come up with your own or select from the list of values provided if they resonate with you. Thinking upon the following may help to trigger values that are most important to you:

- ☐ family, ancestry, and cultural traditions

- ☐ life changing experiences/moments

- ☐ home, school, community, and/or work life

Next, take a few minutes to reflect upon your passions, strongest beliefs, and what is in your heart, then put an asterisk by the seven values from your list that are the most important to you.

Lastly, from your list of seven, put a second asterisk by the three that are the most important.

Once you have your three, give yourself a well-deserved pat on the back—you have determined your most important core values.

Values List

Affluence	Appreciation	Authenticity
Balance	Dependability	Faith
Family	Freedom	Friendship
Happiness	Honesty	Hope
Humility	Influence	Intelligence
Integrity	Justice	Kindness
Love	Mindfulness	Neatness
Peace	Power	Practicality
Preparedness	Realism	Reliability
Security	Service	Spirituality
Status	Success	Tolerance
Trustworthiness	Virtue	Wisdom

Creating S.M.A.R.T. Goals

Specific, **M**easurable, **A**ttainable, **R**elevant, **T**imely

Where there's a *will* there's a *way*. When you establish goals that are meaningful to you, you will find ways and means to achieve them. Your talents, skills, and behavior will rise to meet and conquer the challenges you will undoubtedly face on the way to meeting your goals. When you follow the steps outlined below, you will begin to see clearly what may have once seemed impossible and out of reach

S.M.A.R.T. goals are one of many strategies for goal setting. Follow the S.M.A.R.T. goal instructions below to begin moving into a more fulfilling future. Use the two goals worksheets on the pages that follow to write down your responses, and finally, put your goals into words.

Specific—It is okay to start out with a general goal to begin the process, but specific goals are much more likely to be achieved. To turn a general goal into a specific goal, begin by answering the following questions:

➢ **What** do I want to accomplish?   ➢ **Where** will this take place?

➢ **Why** do I want to accomplish this goal?   ➢ **When** will this happen?

➢ **Who** is involved?   ➢ **Which** requirements and restraints will I face?

Example: A general goal would be, "Become a better public speaker." A specific goal would be, "Take a public speaking course at the local community college this spring."

Measurable—Once the specific goal is established, you are ready to determine the criteria for measuring your progress toward reaching your goal. This keeps you focused and on track to reach target dates. Ask yourself, "how much", "how often", "how many". You may decide to use quantitative data (numbers), or qualitative (descriptive) data to measure your progress.

Example: If your goal is to lose ten pounds, that's quantitative. If it is to wear an outfit you used to fit well, that's descriptive. Both are effective for measuring your progress.

Attainable—Make sure that you make goals that you can attain, otherwise you run the risk of becoming disappointed, and in turn, you are likely to give up. Your goal and your level of commitment should coincide.

Think about the requirements and restraints you identified above. Are you able to fulfill all that is necessary to achieve your goal? Can you overcome any obstacles that may arise? If the answer to either of these questions is "No," you may want to reconsider or tweak your goal. If the answer is "Yes," you're ready to take the next step.

Example: If your goal is to start your own business, make sure you have enough money on hand to pay the bills until your business is up and running, and bringing in a profit. You also want to make sure you have adequate knowledge of the business you plan to open.

Relevant—When determining whether your goal is relevant consider your "Why". It may be tempting to select a goal because it sounds good, but is it really something you would be happy doing?

Example: To become the CEO of a Fortune 500 company sounds very impressive. But if your passion lies in preparing international cuisine and food presentation, it may make more sense to go to a culinary arts school, than to spend enormous amounts of money and time acquiring an MBA degree.

Timely—A goal should always have a time frame. Time frames and deadlines work to motivate people to keep moving toward their goal. Without them, your goal is likely to get lost. It's okay to adjust the time frame when you find that you may not be able to meet it, or if you meet it ahead of time. The point is to have a reasonable time to guide your progress.

Example: If you want to write a book, establish a specific date, month, and year that you want to complete it by. There is a much greater chance that this goal will be achieved when a specific date is attached to it, than if you go on a blind hope that it will eventually be completed.

See the worksheet on the next page.

Creating S.M.A.R.T. Goals Worksheet

Goal	Specific	Measurable	Attainable	Relevant	Time frame
What do you want to achieve?	What? Why? Who? Where? When? Which?	How much? How often? How many?	Is the goal achievable?	Is it important to what you want to achieve ultimately?	What is the time frame, or the deadline set to complete the goal?

Creating S.M.A.R.T. Goals, Continued

Putting your goals into words

Use the area below to put your goals from the worksheet into a statement which describes your goal(s). Include all the components of the worksheet.

Goal 1:

_____

_____

_____

_____

_____

Goal 2:

_____

_____

_____

_____

Goal 3:

_____

_____

_____

_____

Goal 4:

_____

_____

_____

_____

_____

Crafting A Personal Mission Statement

Your personal mission statement conveys your life's purpose. It is the foundation of your motivation. Hence, it should stir up your enthusiasm and excite your passion. It is the cornerstone of your core values. It helps you to design your life purposefully; stay focused; set and achieve goals; and in the process, gain a greater sense of self-agency, self-discipline, and self-respect.

> ➤ **Keep it simple.** Your mission statement should be clear and brief. The best mission statements tend to be three to five sentences long. Some are only one sentence. For instance, a one sentence mission statement might sound like, "Each day I will honor others with my gift of encouragement." It should touch upon what you want to focus on and what kind of person you want to become over the next one to four years.

> ➤ **Keep it positive.** Keep the words in your mission statement positive. It should state what you want to do or become. Not what you don't want to do, or don't want to be.

> ➤ **Keep it specific.** Your mission statement should be specific in actions, behaviors, habits, and qualities that would have a positive impact over a period of time. Include positive life traits, behaviors, and values that you consider important and want to develop further.

A mission statement should guide you in your day-to-day actions and choices. It should be easy to memorize. Repeat it to yourself often, until it rolls off your tongue effortlessly.

Four Step Process to Crafting a Noteworthy Personal Mission Statement

Step One: Make a list of the following:

- ☐ Three to five of your core values, (e.g., accountability, commitment, dedication, education, faith, family, health, honesty, respect, service). Refer to the *Core Values Exercise* in Appendix B.

- ☐ One of your most important long-term goals (e.g., running a triathlon, receiving a doctorate degree), and one short term goal, (e.g., losing five pounds, passing an upcoming exam). Refer to *Creating S.M.A.R.T. Goals* in Appendix B for guidelines on creating goals.

- ☐ Achievements or tasks that you are most proud of. Include achievements or tasks made at home, work, school, church, and/or in the community, (e.g., received a promotion, received an A on a test, led a ministry, volunteered at a homeless shelter).

Step Two: Notice possible themes from the information gathered above, such as, education, leadership, serving others, providing support, and/or giving encouragement.

Step Three: Create your mission statement using the information gathered in steps one and two.

Step Four: Memorize it. Make it succinct and concise so that it is easy to retain.

Example of a personal mission statement: *"Through dedication and grit I will take advantage of opportunities to improve my mind through education, better my body through maintaining a healthy lifestyle, and uplift my community through service."*

Final note: It's essential that your mission statement stays relevant. Your personal mission statement is not meant to be stagnant. It should change and evolve as you grow, improve, and change.

Creating a Vision Board

There is a common belief, "if you can see it, you can achieve it." A vision board helps you do just that—see it. Not only do you see it, but when you take time to look for it, and purposely insert it onto your board, you give clarity and feelings to what you aspire to achieve in your life.

Numerous studies have indicated that when you intentionally surround yourself with images of how you want your life to improve, what career you want to thrive in, where you want to live, where you want to vacation, etc., your life changes to match those images and aspirations.

Supplies needed:

- ☐ Poster board
- ☐ A variety of magazines
- ☐ Scissors
- ☐ Markers, crayons, and/or paint (optional)
- ☐ Glue that won't cause the cutouts to wrinkle, such as rubber cement or glue sticks

Five Easy Steps to Creating a Profound Vision Board:

Step 1: For a deeper experience, prepare yourself mentally with a mindfulness exercise before you begin. Be still, and with an open mind, and positive thinking, ask yourself what you hope to achieve by creating your vision board. Deep breathing, soft music, and a scented candle may help to quiet your mind and keep you focused. (Refer to *Mindfulness Meditations* in Appendix C for more ideas).

Step 2: Go through the magazines, searching for images which jump out at you as something you desire, or someone you admire. Have fun. Tear out whole pages, and cut out pictures, words, and/or headlines that inspire or motivate you. Stack them up and set them aside. You may want to organize your stacks by similarities (e.g., travel, education, exercise). It's up to you.

Step 3: Begin the process of putting the pictures on the board. Don't glue them yet because you may change your mind, adding or eliminating images. That's totally fine. Perhaps you want to organize your board by including themes (e.g., relationships, career, spiritual, physical), or you may lay the images out in a way that narrates a story.

Step 4: After you have all the images on the board in the way that you want them—and that most resonates with your soul—carefully begin to glue them onto your board.

Step 5: Once your board is complete, don't put it out of sight where you can easily forget about it with life's many distractions. Instead, as an artist would value a rare painting, treat it like your masterpiece, and make sure to put it in a place where you will see it often.

Final Note: You can make more than one vision board, especially as you face new challenges, make changes and adjustments in your life, or think of new dreams and goals.

Understanding How Money Grows

Think about this question: Would you rather have $10,000 per day for 30 days or a penny that doubled in value every day for 30 days? Most people might choose the first option, but the correct answer is the second option. The first option will net $300,000.00, and the second option will net more than $5,000,000 dollars! Refer to the compound table below to see how that works.

On the one hand, compounded interest is great, but on the other hand, compounded interest can have adverse effects. For instance, most credit card companies compound interest daily, adding it to the balance at the end of the month. Thus, according to one online calculator, if you only paid the minimum payment on a $15,000.00 balance, at an average interest rate of 14.96%, you would be paying monthly payments for almost 19 years. Moreover, by the time you pay the balance off, you would have paid $27,978.00, which is $12,978.00 over the beginning balance of $15,000.00.

Debt can either make your money grow or shrink. Keep in mind that there is good debt and bad debt. Good debt creates opportunities to grow your money, bad debt has the opposite effect. Simply stated, good debt is anything that will appreciate over time or grow in value, such as property. Bad dept is the opposite, anything that will depreciate over time or lose value, such as food, clothes, vacation. So, as much as possible, make it a rule to use cash instead of credit for the latter items, unless you can pay it off right away.

As your money grows, you are better equipped to save for a rainy day. In case of a financial setback due to job loss or another unforeseen circumstance, experts recommend having an emergency fund with three to six months of expenses at all times. For instance, if your expenses each month are $2,000 x 3 months, you would keep $6,000 in your emergency fund. This gives you up to three months to devise a plan to bring in an adequate amount of income again.

For many, anything having to do with numbers can be daunting. But understanding numbers helps when it comes to making your money work for you, instead of you working for your money. If you haven't already, start saving as soon as possible, regardless of your age. The sooner you begin, the greater the return on your money over time, but it's never too late to start. As one saying goes, *"The best time to plant an oak tree was 20 years ago. The second best time is now."*

The table on the next page is just a demonstration of what happens to a penny doubled over thirty days. This won't happen in the real world of saving and investing given the return on investment today. However, the demonstration shows how investing and/or saving money is almost always a far better option than doing nothing at all.

30-Day Compound Table
Example of a penny doubled over a 30-Day Period

Day 1: $.01	Day 16: $327.68
Day 2: $.02	Day 17: $655.36
Day 3: $.04	Day 18: $1,310.72
Day 4: $.08	Day 19: $2,621.44
Day 5: $.16	Day 20: $5,242.88
Day 6: $.32	Day 21: $10,485.76
Day 7: $.64	Day 22: $20,971.52
Day 8: $1.28	Day 23: $41,943.04
Day 9: $2.56	Day 24: $83,886.08
Day 10: $5.12	Day 25: $167,772.16
Day 11: $10.24	Day 26: $335,544.32
Day 12: $20.48	Day 27: $671,088.64
Day 13: $40.96	Day 28: $1,342,177.28
Day 14: $81.92	Day 29: $2,684,354.56
Day 15: $163.84	Day 30: $5,368,709.12

Time Management Skills

The individual who can efficiently manage their time is the one who is also more likely to effectively manage their life. After all, discipline and self-control are two powerful behavior attributes of time management—which are also two critical components of life management. Without these components, circumstances may spiral out of control more often than not.

Face it, anyone can be late. But it takes scrutiny, diligence, and self-mastery to be on time. The individual who possesses these qualities is already ahead of the game. The following exercise, *Work Backwards to Stay Ahead*, is a strategy for sharpening time management skills when it comes to arriving on time.

Work Backwards to Stay Ahead

To ensure that you're on time every time, the first thing to remember is, *if you're on time, you're late*. Therefore, plan accordingly to always arrive at least 10 minutes ahead of time for appointments, all the way to two hours ahead of time for air travel. The next thing to do is, *work your way backwards*. The following steps will get you there on time, every time—poised, confident, and stress free.

Let's say you have an appointment at 10 a.m.

- ☐ First, the day before the appointment, ask yourself what your travel time will be. How long will it take to arrive, door to door, by 9:50 a.m. so that you are there 10 minutes early? **(Example: travel time = 15 minutes)**.

- ☐ Second, add cushion-time for any unforeseeable delays, such as forgetting your phone; traffic, getting gas, or finding a parking space **(Example: cushion time = 15 minutes + travel time = 15 minutes for a total of 30 minutes)**. That tells you that you have to be out the door by 9:20 a.m. for a 9:50 a.m. arrival time.

- ☐ Next, as you continue working your way backward, ask yourself how long it will take to get dressed **(Time to get dressed = 1 hour)**. Hence, you would need to begin getting dressed by 8:20 a.m. to be out the door by 9:20 a.m.

- ☐ Last, ask yourself how long it takes to complete any other necessary tasks before getting dressed for the appointment, e.g., eating, exercising, walking the dog, hitting the snooze button **(Miscellaneous time = 1 hour)**.

In this example, to get to your appointment comfortably and on time, you would need to begin getting ready by 7:20 a.m. This would allow 2 hours and 30 minutes to prepare to be out the door by 9:20 a.m., arriving for your 10:00 a.m. appointment—poised, confident, and stress free.

10 Tips for Developing Steadfast Skills in Time Management

1. Continually look for ways to free up time to allow for more time to take care of yourself. In other words, work smarter not harder. Perhaps you delegate responsibilities whenever possible or organize items (files, mail, clothes) so that items you need are found promptly.

2. Acknowledge unproductive habits and find ways to change or eliminate them. Be mindful of when you may be caught up in an unproductive project and stop as soon as possible.

3. Try to use waiting time wisely and productively. For instance, you can use idle time to review notes, read, rehearse, study, do deep breathing, or practice developing patience.

4. When you catch yourself procrastinating, ask yourself, "What am I avoiding?"

5. Break projects down into small steps, then start with the most difficult step first, focusing your attention on one thing at a time.

6. Put most of your efforts and time in areas that provide long-term gain.

7. Prioritize obligations. Trust your judgment on the order. Once you set your priorities, stick to them.

8. Plan your day each morning, or the night before, and make a "to-do" list to keep on track. Set deadlines whenever possible.

9. Evaluate your progress at the end of each day. Reward yourself as you complete items, especially the most important tasks.

10. Count all of your time as time to be used well by making deliberate attempts to get satisfaction out of every moment possible.

Remember the following words of wisdom:

☐ Idle time is the devil's workshop.

☐ If you're on time, you're late.

☐ There is no such thing as "Fashionably late."

Sample S.W.O.R. Analysis©   By Dr. Sarah Washington O'Neal Rush

Name: _____James Smith_____ **Date:** 1/1/2025 _____

Desired Area to Grow and Improve: _____Getting past fear of public speaking_____

1. On a scale of **1** to **10**, with **1** being **not at all confident** in conquering this area of growth and improvement, and **10** being **highly confident** to conquer this, where are you right now? _5_

2. Use the boxes on the next page to briefly brainstorm a few answers to the questions below:

(See examples below questions for area of ***getting past fear of public speaking***)

S—Self-Assurance

- ☐ **What are you most sure about in terms of the area you want to conquer?**
  Example: *I have something important to say.*

- ☐ **Where are you most sustainable or steadfast?**
  Example: *People value my opinion.*

- ☐ **What is the evidence of this?**
  Example: *People often ask for my input.*

- ☐ **What are the results?**
  Example: *They are inspired and encouraged.*

W—Worries

- ☐ **What are your fears/What is the worst thing that can happen?**
  Example: *I will fumble on my words. I'll leave something important out.*

- ☐ **What evidence supports this?**
  Example: *It's happened before. There is no evidence.*

- ☐ **What can you do about your fears and/or evidence?**
  Example: *Positive self-talk. Take public speaking classes. Use note cards.*

- ☐ **What might the results be?**
  Example: *Reduced levels of stress and anxiety. Increased confidence.*

O—Options

☐ **What is available now to get to where you want to be?**
Example: *Join Toastmasters. Making time to rehearse.*

☐ **What is in the way of what is available/What can you do about it?**
Example: *Procrastination. Time. Get up earlier. Find creative ways to rehearse, in the car, in waiting rooms.*

☐ **What is most sustainable from what is available?**
Example: *Toastmasters provides ample support and feedback. Rehearsal preps me for great delivery.*

☐ **What are the steps to attain what is available?**
Example: *Intentionality of thought. Sign up for Toastmasters. Write an outline to begin practicing.*

R—Risks > Rewards > Readiness

☐ **What are the potential risks?**
Example: *Leaving out important information. Not being invited back.*

☐ **What can you do about the potential risks?**
Example: *Move on to the next opportunity. Continue to practice and get better.*

☐ **What are the potential rewards?**
Example: *Getting the majority of intended message out. Inspiring and encouraging others.*

☐ **Do the rewards outweigh the risks, or vice versa?**
Example: *Yes!* (If *No*, perhaps it's time to move on and find a new area to grow and improve in.)

S.W.O.R. Preliminary Analysis©

By Dr. Sarah Washington O'Neal Rush

Name: _____   Date: _____

Desired area to grow and improve:_____

1. On a scale of **1** to **10**, with **1** being **not at all confident** in conquering this area of growth and improvement, and **10** being **highly confident** to conquer this, where are you right now?_____

2. Use the boxes on the next page to briefly brainstorm a few answers to the questions below:

S—Self-Assurance

☐ **What are you most sure about in terms of the area you want to conquer?**

☐ **Where are you most sustainable or steadfast?**

☐ **What is the evidence of this?**

☐ **What are the results?**

W—Worries

☐ **What are your fears/What is the worst thing that can happen?**

☐ **What evidence supports this?**

☐ **What can you do about your fears and/or evidence?**

☐ **What might the results be?**

O—Options

☐ **What is available now to get to where you want to be?**

☐ **What is in the way of what is available/What can you do about it?**

☐ **What is most sustainable from what is available?**

☐ **What are the steps to attain what is available?**

R—Risks>Rewards>Readiness

☐ **What are the potential risks?**

☐ **What can you do about the potential risks?**

☐ **What are the potential rewards?**

☐ **Do the rewards outweigh the risks, or vice versa?**

S. W. O. R. Assessment Chart©

Self-Assurance	Worries
Options	Risk>Rewards>Readiness

On a scale of 1 to 10, with 1 being highly dissatisfied and 10 being highly satisfied, how do you feel about where you are in each category?

S. W. O. R. Scale©	In the Beginning	Desired by the End	Actual by the End
Self-Assurance			
Worries			
Options			
Readiness			

Answer the following after you have completed all three pages of this analysis:

On a scale of **1** to **10**, with **1** being **not at all confident** in conquering this area of growth and improvement, and **10** being **highly confident** to conquer this, where are you right now?_____
If the number is less than 10, what would it take for you to move up by 1, 2, 3…?)
If the number is more than 1, why isn't it lower?)

(Use the blank space below to record your thoughts)

S. W. O. R. Analysis 3-Step Action Plan©

Step One

What:
_____

_____

How:
_____

_____

When:
_____

_____

Step Two

What:
_____

_____

How:
_____

_____

When:
_____

_____

Step Three

What:
_____

_____

How:
_____

_____

When:
_____

_____

S.W.O.R. Post Analysis©

By Dr. Sarah Washington O'Neal Rush

Name: _____   Date: _____

Desired area to grow and improve:_____

3. On a scale of 1 to 10, with 1 being not at all confident in conquering this area of growth and improvement, and 10 being highly confident to conquer this, where are you right now?_____

4. Use the boxes on the next page to briefly brainstorm a few answers to the questions below:

S—Self-Assurance

☐ **What are you most sure about in terms of the area you want to conquer?**

☐ **Where are you most sustainable or steadfast?**

☐ **What is the evidence of this?**

☐ **What are the results?**

W—Worries

☐ **What are your fears/What is the worst thing that can happen?**

☐ **What evidence supports this?**

☐ **What can you do about your fears and/or evidence?**

☐ **What might the results be?**

O—Options

☐ **What is available now to get to where you want to be?**

☐ **What is in the way of what is available/What can you do about it?**

☐ **What is most sustainable from what is available?**

☐ **What are the steps to attain what is available?**

R—Risks>Rewards>Readiness

☐ **What are the potential risks?**

☐ **What can you do about the potential risks?**

☐ **What are the potential rewards?**

☐ **Do the rewards outweigh the risks, or vice versa?**

Self-Assurance	Worries

Options	Risk>Rewards>Readiness

On a scale of 1 to 10, with 1 being highly dissatisfied and 10 being highly satisfied, how do you feel about where you are in each category?

S. W. O. R. Scale©	In the Beginning	Desired by the End	Actual by the End
Self-Assurance			
Worries			
Options			
Readiness			

Answer the following after you have completed all three pages of this analysis:

On a scale of **1** to **10**, with **1** being **not at all confident** in conquering this area of growth and improvement, and **10** being **highly confident** to conquer this, where are you right now?
If the number is less than 10, what would it take for you to move up by 1, 2, 3. . .?)_____
If the number is more than 1, why isn't it lower?)

(Use the blank space below to record your thoughts)

S. W. O. R. Analysis 3-Step Action Plan©

Step One

What: _____

_____

How: _____

_____

When: _____

_____

Step Two

What: _____

_____

How: _____

_____

When: _____

_____

Step Three

What: _____

_____

How: _____

_____

When: _____

_____

S.W.O.R. Analysis©

By Dr. Sarah Washington O'Neal Rush

Name: _____   Date:_____

Desired area to grow and improve:_____

5. On a scale of **1** to **10**, with **1** being **not at all confident** in conquering this area of growth and improvement, and **10** being **highly confident** to conquer this, where are you right now?_____

6. Use the boxes on the next page to briefly brainstorm a few answers to the questions below:

S—Self-Assurance

☐ **What are you most sure about in terms of the area you want to conquer?**

☐ **Where are you most sustainable or steadfast?**

☐ **What is the evidence of this?**

☐ **What are the results?**

W—Worries

☐ **What are your fears/What is the worst thing that can happen?**

☐ **What evidence supports this?**

☐ **What can you do about your fears and/or evidence?**

☐ **What might the results be?**

O—Options

☐ **What is available now to get to where you want to be?**

☐ **What is in the way of what is available/What can you do about it?**

☐ **What is most sustainable from what is available?**

☐ **What are the steps to attain what is available?**

R—Risks>Rewards>Readiness

☐ **What are the potential risks?**

☐ **What can you do about the potential risks?**

☐ **What are the potential rewards?**

☐ **Do the rewards outweigh the risks, or vice versa?**

S. W. O. R. Assessment Chart©

Self-Assurance	Worries

Options	Risk>Rewards>Readiness

On a scale of 1 to 10, with 1 being highly dissatisfied and 10 being highly satisfied, how do you feel about where you are in each category?

S. W. O. R. Scale©	In the Beginning	Desired by the End	Actual by the End
Self-Assurance			
Worries			
Options			
Readiness			

Answer the following after you have completed all three pages of this analysis:

On a scale of **1** to **10**, with **1** being **not at all confident** in conquering this area of growth and improvement, and **10** being **highly confident** to conquer this, where are you right now?_____
If the number is less than 10, what would it take for you to move up by 1, 2, 3…?)
If the number is more than 1, why isn't it lower?)

(Use the blank space below to record your thoughts)

S. W. O. R. Analysis 3-Step Action Plan©

Step One

What: _____

_____

How: _____

_____

When: _____

Step Two

What: _____

_____

How: _____

_____

When: _____

_____

Step Three

What: _____

_____

How: _____

_____

When: _____

_____

Appendix C
Mindset & Self-Awareness

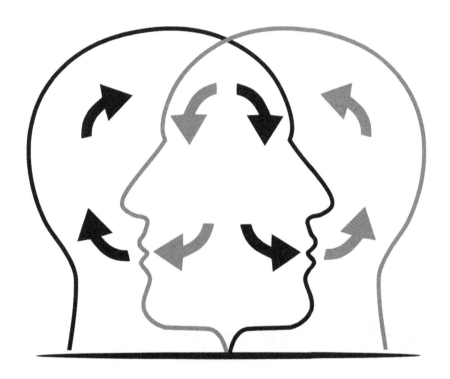

Mindset Awareness: Growth versus Fixed

Studies find that there are two mindsets, fixed and growth, and that individuals tend to move along a continuum, back and forth between the two. The fixed mindset is the belief that basic characteristics, talent, abilities, and intelligence are fixed traits. Whereas a growth mindset is the belief that these traits can be developed and improved upon over time.

According to the research, individuals with growth mindsets tend to have much more success in life than those with fixed mindsets. However, they may have growth mindsets in one area, and fixed mindsets in another. For example, one may be confident that with diligence and hard work, they can ace a math test. But this same person may believe there is no amount of practice that can make them a better public speaker.

How do we move toward the further end of the growth continuum? Good question. According to the founding psychologist of this work, Carol Dweck, since mindsets are beliefs, though they are powerful, with intention they can be changed.

Seven Tips to move from a fixed to a growth mindset:

1. Identify areas where you have a fixed mindset, e.g., test taking, growing a business, being assertive, staying on budget.

2. Choose to do something about it.

3. Find the opportunity in the difficulty.

4. Learn from mistakes, realizing that everyone makes them.

5. Change the language you use from "I never" to "I haven't yet."

6. Hang around others who possess growth mindsets.

7. Never give up.

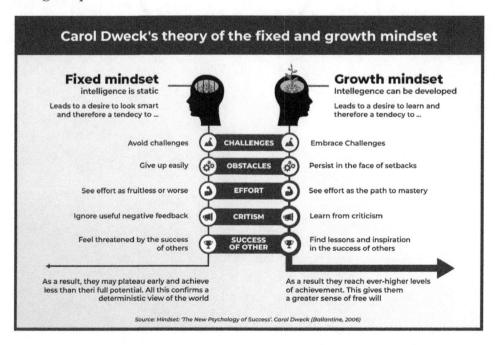

Reframing Negative Self-Talk into Positive Self-Affirmations

We must be mindful of what we say when we talk to ourselves. Our internal dialogue, or self-talk, is something we engage in much more than we may realize. Developing awareness of these internal conversations is especially important because far too often, negative self-talk is on "auto-pilot," while positive self-talk is on the "back-burner," at best. Negative self-talk is the predecessor of much of our behaviors and our decisions. As such, it is one of the most self-destructive and dangerous habits we have.

The following exercise will help bring awareness to how often we may engage in negative self-talk, and thereby allow us to replace negative statements with positive affirmations. The goal of this exercise is to make us aware of our self-criticisms in order to create positive self-talk and improve upon how we think of ourselves.

1. First, on a blank sheet of paper, list everything you like about yourself—strengths, positive personality traits, abilities, gifts, talents, appearance, things that you often receive compliments on, etc.

2. Next, on a second blank sheet of paper, list all the things you don't like about yourself—perceived weaknesses, negative characteristics, appearance, etc.

3. Review the second list, and on a new blank sheet of paper, write a positive version for each negative item. The new version should be supportive and encouraging. For instance, the following statement, "I am socially incompetent around people I don't know," might be restated as, "I am reserved until I feel comfortable around people who I am unfamiliar with." Be sure that the new version is true. At times you may have to be resourceful to get to the positive thought.

4. When you are finished, destroy the list of negatives. This allows you to symbolically release the negatives. Keep your original list of positives and your reframed list. Review from time to time. This will keep your self-esteem in check.

A final thought, as the saying goes, "habits are meant to be broken." For the purposes of this workbook, the only habits we are concerned about breaking are the negative, unhealthy, bad habits. When it comes to negative self-talk, the good news is that we have a choice. We can decide on what we say to ourselves. The reverse of negative self-talk is positive self-affirmations, or positive self-talk. As with any habit, developing a habit of positive self-talk is going to have a powerful influence on the way we think.

Self-fulfilling Prophecy and the Law of Suggestion

Your subconscious mind does not think for itself. It is highly responsive to suggestion—believing whatever is impressed upon it. It doesn't compare and contrast, or reason, as the conscious mind does. If you provide it with wrong information, it will accept it as true and then proceed to bring the information to fruition. Thus, many personal life experiences result from thoughts impressed on the subconscious mind through belief.

The subconscious mind responds to a person's conscious thoughts without trying to analyze whether those thoughts are negative or positive, or right or wrong. It simply accepts whatever the conscious mind believes. In other words, if on a conscious level one believes that they are inadequate to complete a certain task, their subconscious mind will confirm that by psychologically undermining the person's actual ability. As a result, they are likely to fail at the task. Creating a *self-fulfilling prophecy*. By the same token, if on a conscious level, one believes they can succeed at the task, they are more likely to succeed. As Henry Ford so adequately put it, *"Whether you think you can, or think you can't, you're right."*

Habits are products of the subconscious, as they develop from conscious habitual thinking which establishes deep grooves in the subconscious mind. If habitual thoughts are harmonious, peaceful, and constructive, positive habits will develop. On the other hand, when negative ideas are consistently conveyed to the subconscious mind, negative habits develop, which can overflow into other parts of your life. For instance, if you consciously dwell on a relationship that ended badly, you are likely to create a bad internal mood which will overflow into negative experiences in other relationships, perhaps with classmates, coworkers, family and/or friends.

You can overcome these negative experiences with frequent repetition of positive, constructive thoughts. As you do this, your subconscious mind begins to accept the new thought patterns you are developing. Subsequently, you are allowing new and healthy habits of thinking to form. Complete the exercise below to see how easily repetition can influence the mind.

Power of Suggestion Exercise:

We can't get away from advertisements. Advertising is big business. A 30-second commercial during the 2023 Super Bowl cost $7 million dollars. There's a reason companies are willing to pay this—because the power of suggestion is *powerful and profitable*. Most of the time viewers watch and listen to commercials mindlessly, while the intended suggestion from the message seeps into their subconscious, over and over and over. Try the following exercise:

Quickly spell coke (c-o-k-e) immediately followed by saying the word coke. Then immediately answer the question in #2.

For example: Say "C-o-k-e, Coke" four times quickly and effortlessly without thinking about it.

Repeat the chant in #1 below quickly and mindlessly four times in a row. Then quickly read and answer the question in #2.

1. "Coke, c-o-k-e. "Coke, c-o-k-e. "Coke, c-o-k-e. "Coke, c-o-k-e."

2. What is the outer part of a boiled egg called?

What was your answer to number 2?
(See next page for correct answer)

Answer to Power of Suggestion Exercise:

If you followed directions without taking time to think about it or looking ahead to the answer, and you said **yolk**, you're like most people—unfortunately, you're incorrect.

If, without taking time to think about it or looking ahead to the answer, you said **albumen** or **shell**, go to the top of your class. You're likely an analytical thinker, and not one who can be easily influenced.

Considering that most people will say yolk when the exercise is done correctly, demonstrates how easy it is for repeated clever messages to get into our psyches and influence our thoughts. This demonstration took less than five minutes of our time. Think about how many messages we hear over and over, and what type of impact that can have.

Finally, before buying into everyone else's message, ask yourself the following questions:

1. What's in it for them if I buy into their message?

2. What's in it for me?

3. Does it meet the logical sense test?

4. How will believing this make my life better?

5. In the long run, does it provide the greatest good for the greater number of people?

Reversing Irrational Thoughts Exercise

It may seem that events in our lives cause our feelings, and in turn affect our actions. But the truth is, it's what we tell ourselves about a particular event that impacts our feelings, and in turn affects our behavior. If the events in our lives caused our feelings, the same event would cause the same feelings in everyone. The steps below are based on Rational Emotive Behavior Theory, which provides tools that can be used every day to help control seemingly unmanageable thoughts, feelings, and behaviors.

Exercise:

1. Remember a time when you experienced negative feelings. Perhaps you felt frustrated, angry, embarrassed, or out of control. Write down the **event** that came before the feeling. An event is something you can record or take a picture of, such as an extremely slow moving line when you are in a hurry.

2. Next, identify the **thoughts** that preceded the feelings. Write these thoughts down in detail. For example, "This only happens when I am in a hurry," "This only happens to me," "I may get fired if I am late again." Only list your thoughts.

3. Next, write down the **feelings** that resulted from the thoughts. For instance, feelings of anger, frustration, worry, stress, etc.

4. Next, write down the **behaviors** (your actions) which followed these feelings. For instance: screaming, making obscene gestures or remarks, blowing the horn, cursing, etc.

5. Lastly, go back to the negative thoughts. Challenge these irrational thoughts by replacing them with helpful, healthier, and more realistic thoughts. For example:

   a. You might say, "This too shall pass," or "I can use the time to think of how to organize the rest of my day," or "I can do simple meditation exercises like paying attention to my breathing as I deliberately take slow, deep inhales, and slow, purposeful exhales."

   b. If you are stuck in traffic, you might think, "Maybe getting stuck helped me to avoid an accident." You can also listen to educational or motivational audio books or podcasts while in your car and turn the time into a personal development opportunity. The longer you are stuck in the traffic jam, the more you will gain by simply changing your thinking and therefore, your actions.

Ultimately, once you get the basics down—identify the **event**, identify your **thoughts**, identify your **feelings** (anger, frustration, loneliness, depression, insecure, scared, etc.), you can alter your **behavior** from negative, unhealthy, and destructive, to positive, healthy, and constructive, as you apply this tool in the real world.

Mindfulness Meditations

Mindfulness is the practice of focusing your attention on the present. We can practice mindfulness in every experience—from eating, to showering, to walking, to waiting (i.e., in line, in traffic, on hold, or during commercials) and more. Some believe it's difficult to meditate, however, if you are able to worry, you are able to meditate. Worry is dwelling on negative future possibilities, whereas, meditation is dwelling on peace, regardless of present or possible future circumstances.

Mindfulness leads to excellence. Practicing mindfulness helps the body to de-stress. Thus, you can think more clearly, and make better decisions.

The following mindful exercises are simple to do, yet powerful for relieving stress and anxiety, or simply for gaining peace of mind. Before beginning a mindfulness meditation exercise, take a few deep breaths to help you begin to bring yourself into the present moment.

- ☐ **Breathing:** Count slowly to four as you inhale, hold for a slow count of four, and slowly count to four again as you exhale. Do this four times in a row. Pay close attention to what your breath feels like—feel the sensations of each breath as they flow in and out of your body. Notice the sensations in your rib cage, stomach, belly button, nostrils, and shoulders.

- ☐ **Grounding:** Sit still with both feet flat on the floor and hands open by your side or resting in your lap. With your eyes opened or closed, mentally focus on how your body feels, beginning from the soles of your feet, and moving along your entire body until you reach the top of your head. Work your way back to the soles of your feet.

- ☐ **Experiential Eating:** Before putting your food in your mouth, pay attention to its appearance. While eating, pay close attention to your other sensory experiences—taste, texture, and smell.

- ☐ **In the Shower:** When taking a shower, intentionally notice how the water feels as it hits your body, and how it feels rolling down. Notice the temperature and the sound.

- ☐ **Listening to Music:** Listen to a favorite song and pay close attention to how it makes you feel; what emotions get stirred up; what memories come up; and how those memories make you feel. Stay with the emotions for at least one minute after the song ends and see where they lead.

- ☐ **In Stolen Moments:** Before checking to see who called, what's on television, or what's going on in social media, take a minute to purposely seek out things that are not man-made, (e.g., trees, birds, the sky, clouds, flowers, mountains, how the wind moves through the air as indicated by the movement of leaves, etc.).

- ☐ **Melting:** Sit and relax and imagine yourself melting into everything around you. Do this for at least one minute and notice your feelings.

- ☐ **In Silence:** Spend at least two minutes in silence, taking in the atmosphere around you.

- ☐ **Watching the Flame:** Stare at a candle flame for at least one minute while paying attention to everything about it. When your mind wanders, intentionally bring it back to the flame.

On a final note, over time, raise the bar by increasing your meditation time. And remember, if you know how to worry, you know how to meditate. Dwelling on the positive rather than the negative is the key.

Personality: Uncomplicating the Complicated

The American Psychological Association defines personality as *enduring characteristics and behavior that comprise a person's unique adjustment to life*. There are numerous other variations to this definition that can be found online—which confirms the complexity of this psychological construct. Since our lives are largely impacted by this intriguing force, especially in relationship to how our personality interacts with the unique personalities of others, the following sections, *Personality—Id, Ego, and Superego; Personality—Common Defense Mechanisms;* and *Personality and Perception*, attempt to make this phenomenon a bit easier to understand. Consequently, understanding is a great first step toward cultivating peace in relationships.

Personality—Id, Ego, and Superego

According to the founder of psychoanalysis, Sigmund Freud, the id, ego, and superego are three inner forces that make up the human personality. Freud asserted that the combination of these three forces working together explains the complexity of human behavior. Accordingly, the id generates demands, the ego in turn represents reason and reality, and the superego interjects moral thinking into the resulting responses and/or actions.

Id: Pleasure Seeking

The id is the most primitive part of the personality and seeks instant gratification for our wants and needs. If they go unmet, aggravation, anxiety, or anger may ensue.

Examples Include:

☐ A baby cries until their diaper is changed.

☐ A toddler displays a temper tantrum in the store when his mom refused to buy him a toy.

☐ An irate driver runs their car into a car that cut them off on the freeway.

Ego: Reality Seeking

The ego is concerned with reality. Its goal is to accommodate the desires of the id in a manner that is deemed socially appropriate. The ego is considerate of what others think. It involves discipline and impulse control as it works to eliminate the negative feelings brought on by the id.

Examples Include:

☐ A woman was so exhausted during a meeting at work, she wanted to lay across the conference room table and go to sleep. To save herself embarrassment, she drank a strong cup of coffee, and waited for her break to take a catnap in her private office.

☐ A patient was so afraid after learning that he needed a tetanus shot, he imagined himself running out of the doctor's office before the nurse came in to give the injection. Instead, in order to maintain his dignity, he decided to quietly follow the doctor's orders.

☐ A young man's father let him borrow the car to go to the library to study for an exam. On the way he saw friends who said they were going to a nearby sporting event. Though tempted, he chose to head to the library and not take a chance on failing the exam and upsetting his father.

Superego: Morality Seeking

The superego is the last force to develop. Its concern is morality, doing the right thing, and avoiding wrongdoing at all cost. The decisions of the ego and superego often draw the same conclusions about what action to take. The difference between them is that the ego is concerned with consequences and what others think, and the superego is concerned with values and principles.

Examples Include:

☐ When a shopper arrived at her car, she realized she didn't pay for an item that was at the bottom of her cart. She was aware that she'd gotten out of the store without anyone noticing. She thought about keeping the item and leaving, but instead decided to return it to the store clerk.

☐ A bank customer was given twenty dollars over the amount he requested. He was experiencing financial difficulties and thought about chalking the extra money up to a blessing. After giving it more thought, and realizing the teller would be short at the end of the day, he made the decision to give the money back.

☐ After learning that she was the one who actually broke the office printer that she'd accused her coworker of breaking, the employee thought about keeping the truth to herself. Upon seeing the disappointment on her coworker's face because she thought she broke the printer, the accusing employee came forward with the truth.

Though the decisions that result from the ego and superego are often in alignment, the demands of the id are often in conflict with the demands of the ego and superego. When this occurs, the ego tends to deal with it by operating unconscious defense mechanisms. Read on.

Personality—Common Defense Mechanisms

Defense mechanisms emerged from Sigmund Freud's personality theory. They are most often learned behaviors developed in childhood. They are unconscious coping strategies used by the ego to protect us from anxiety caused by unpleasant and painful emotions. Since they are learned, we can choose to learn healthier coping strategies that will be much more beneficial to us.

As you read the following list of some of the most common defense mechanisms, you may find that you are familiar with them in yourself, or in others. Understanding, recognizing, and acknowledging problem behavior is half the battle, and an excellent first step to adopting healthier coping skills.

Primitive Defense Mechanisms

The following four **Primitive Defense Mechanisms** begin to develop in the earliest stages of life. Yet, if unacknowledged, can wreak havoc in the later stages of life.

1. **Denial:** Denial is when a person will not accept the fact that something which is true, is actually true. A common example of denial is a friend who does not pick up on signs that a friendship is over, or an alcoholic who insist they have control over drinking, or when someone doesn't accept that a loved one is terminally ill.

2. **Projection:** Projection occurs when someone thinks that someone else is experiencing the same thoughts and feelings that they think and feel. This especially occurs when the thoughts and feelings are believed to be unacceptable by family, friends, or society. Admitting these thoughts and feelings can cause tremendous emotional pain. Hence, projecting them away from self and onto others in an effort to avoid the pain. Envy, anger, bitterness, and hatred are often projected.

3. **Reaction Formation:** Reaction formation is when someone reacts intensely to their own undisclosed desires or behaviors by attempting to harshly critique those same behaviors in others. Examples include someone who goes out of their way to shower kindness on someone they secretly despise. Or a person who lectures those who go out to bars, yet they drink heavily at home, behind closed doors. Or someone who fights against capitalism, while earning millions from their own private business.

4. **Acting Out:** Acting out happens when someone displays their feelings through inappropriate behavior because they are unable to properly express their feelings. It's a way of physically venting in order to rid themselves of emotional pain. An example of acting out is self-mutilation or cutting behavior. The physical pain serves as a distraction to the emotional pain, which often feels worse. Another example is when someone who feels rejected behaves badly in order to attract attention.

Less Primitive Defense Mechanisms

The following four Less **Primitive Defense Mechanisms** are considered more mature than primitive defense mechanisms. These defense mechanisms are mostly adopted in adulthood. Though they may not cause as much disturbance in our life as the primitive mechanisms, they are still not ideal coping strategies.

1. **Displacement:** Displacement occurs when someone takes their frustration out on someone other than the person who caused the frustration. For instance, an employee who is upset because her boss yelled at her, contains her anger until she gets home. At home she yells uncontrollably at her son for accidentally spilling water on the floor. This is because her son presents less of a threat than her boss.

2. **Intellectualization:** Intellectualization is a means of separating ourselves from unwanted emotions by thinking about situations in an academic, logical way. For example, someone who experiences a tragic loss of a loved one may begin to put all of their energy into learning about death and the afterlife so that they distance themselves from their feelings and emotions about the loss.

3. **Rationalization:** Rationalization involves logically explaining undesirable circumstances or behaviors by making excuses and/or blaming external forces, rather than taking personal responsibility. For instance, an employee is fired for excessive absences and says that they were fired because their boss never liked them. Or a team member who doesn't put in anywhere near as much time as the other players, accuses the coach of favoritism when they are not allowed as much playing time as the others.

4. **Undoing:** Undoing occurs when someone attempts to correct, or balance out, poor behavior by overcompensating with good behavior. For example, a customer yells at their server when their food arrives cold, and afterwards begins overly commending them about their service.

Personality and Perception

"It's not what you look at that matters, it's what you see." ~Henry David Thoreau

Perceptions about our circumstances are more important than the circumstance itself because different people can perceive the exact same situation differently. In turn, they will assign different meanings to it. For example, a roller coaster ride is the same every time; the only variable is the experience of the individual riding the roller coaster. Individual experiences range from feelings of pure ecstasy to feelings of complete terror. Our life's experiences not only shape and mold our perceptions, but they also form our personality.

Whether conscious or unconscious, our view of the world around us is colored by a combination of life events. This is how perceptions are developed. Some people believe that our perception begins to develop in the womb. That's why expectant mothers sometimes read, talk, and sing to their unborn baby. For certain, perspective begins to form as soon as a child is born. In the womb they are automatically fed, and they are not uncomfortable with soiled diapers. Once babies are born, they are often in a measure of distress until they are fed and changed. As you can imagine, the length of time that it takes, and the frequency of positive and/or negative experiences in getting these primary needs met, is going to have an impact on a child's perception about whether life is good and safe or bad and dangerous.

As our perceptions follow us from our childhood to our teen years, and on to adulthood, they become further imbedded in our psyche, and different mindsets begin to settle in. They can determine whether we will have a good day or a bad day. This awareness of how perception, personality, and mindsets develop can go a long way toward breeding tolerance, understanding, and the ability to get along with others. This same awareness in ourselves can help us to change deeply imbedded mindsets which hold us back from living our highest quality of life. When we change negative mindsets, we can change destructive perceptions.

Look at the images below to get a hands-on view of perception. If working alone, after seeing the first image that comes into view, try to see the other image that is also there. If working in a group, describe what you see in each of the images. Others in the group are likely to see a different image than you may see.

Image One: What do you see?

Source: By Diarb2008 (Own work) [CC BY-SA 3.0
(http://creativecommons.org/licenses/by-sa/3.0)],
via Wikimedia Commons

Image Two: What do you see?

Source: Popular Science Monthly Volume 54
(Jastrow, Joseph: "The Mind's Eye", p.299-312)
Date: 1899

See the following page for an explanation of the above images.

Explanation of Images in Perception Exercise

In **Image One**, some people see five chess pieces, while others see two exact images of two women facing one another with their heads tilted slightly downward.

In **Image Two**, some see a rabbit with long ears, while others see a duck with a long beak.

The pictures haven't changed. We just emphasize different parts of it and assign different meanings. We fill in a lot of blanks with our minds. If we have incomplete perceptions—which we practically always have to some extent—our minds fill in the rest.

The meaning of something will change when you look at it differently. You can look at anything from a fresh new perspective and it will take on a new identity. You can always choose to change interpretations of what you perceive. Why not choose to be positive?

On a final note, when it comes to personality, different people have different life experiences that have gone into shaping their behavior and their personality. The information here only scratches the surface of how personalities develop and why no two people see the world the same. With that in mind, the following statement, graciously explains why we should be careful not to judge:

"Try never to judge. The human mind is so delicate and so complex that only its Maker can know it wholly. Each mind is so different, actuated by such different motives, controlled by such different circumstances, influenced by such different experiences; you cannot know all the influences that have gone in to [a mind]to make up a personality. Therefore, it is impossible to wholly judge that personality."
—**Author Unknown**

Excellence Inventory

The purpose of this exercise is to empower you to counter and control the negative internal voice that you will undoubtedly encounter from time to time. This voice tends to undermine and interrupt the flow of positive growth.

Take inventory of your essential qualities, those you have and those you are striving toward. Just by writing these qualities down, you will elevate your mind and your spirit.

Examples:　　**In excellence** I am working diligently to achieve my dreams.

　　　　　　　　In excellence I am always going to keep my word.

　　　　　　　　In excellence I am going to complete what I start.

　　　　　　　　In excellence I am choosing not to gossip, criticize, or judge.

When making your list, ensure that it is extensive. Consider important areas of your life where you want to improve on something, such as: health, education, work, home, relationships, emotions, finances, etc.

For a more substantial experience, make two copies of your completed sentences. Laminate one and put it in a place where you will see it often, and carry the other one around so that you can always refer to it.

In terms of your qualities, complete the following sentences:

In excellence I am _____

In excellence I am _____

In excellence I am _____

In excellence I am _____

In excellence I am _____

In excellence I am _____

In excellence I am _____

In excellence I am _____

In excellence I am _____

In excellence I am _____

Tracing Your Genealogy

While there are several great tools available to assist in tracing family genealogy, Ancestry.com, will be demonstrated here because they provide an extensive list of material for free. However, to see full results and scanned images of original records, you must utilize the paid "subscriber-only" pages of the website. Once you become familiar centers, with searching the available free databases, you may decide to advance to the paid "subscriber-only" database. Some establishments, such as, libraries and LDS family history centers, allow visitors access to databases which provide full results and scanned images of original records at no cost.

The Ancestry.com website provides a wealth of information. At the time of this writing there were over 9 billion records and more than 30,000 databases; all available US census records for the years 1790 through 1940; many English, Canadian, and Welsh records; city directories, yearbooks, and newspapers from as early as the 1700s; over 20,000 digitized family and local history books; military records from both World Wars, and the Revolutionary and Civil wars; and immigration records, including passenger lists from US ports and border crossings. The following steps will get you started on your way to learning your family history.

Seven Simple Steps to Begin Searching Your Family Genealogy with Ancestry.com:

1. Create your family tree

First, type https://secure.ancestry.com/register/index/ in the web browser. Follow the instructions to create your guest account. Once you have logged into your guest account, you will be able to create your family tree, explore thousands of records, and share information with other users.

Next, from the Home page under the Trees link, select Create and Manage Trees, and then click on Start a New Tree. There you will find an undeveloped pedigree chart which allows you to input your information. Always use surnames when entering name data. If you have already created your tree in another program such as Family Tree Maker, or if you have a GEDCOM file (a universal family tree file format), you may simply upload your file. After you have created your tree, whenever you log into Ancestry.com and sign on to your account, your tree will be available. In addition to your family tree, you may also create additional trees (e.g., your spouse's tree, your paternal side of your family, etc.).

2. Pay attention to the hints

Whenever a leaf icon appears in the ancestor's box, it means Ancestry.com has provided a hint for you to explore. All your hints can be found under the Tree Pages drop down menu at the top of the page. Some hints will apply to your family members, and some will not. You can either view the record or view a comparison between the hint and what is in your tree. You may dismiss the ones that do not apply by clicking ignore, or select the ones that apply by putting a check next to it, and then click Save to Your Tree to import the information. Some records can only be seen by subscribing to a paid Ancestry.com account.

3. Search one family member and one category at a time

To avoid being inundated and overwhelmed with the tons of information that Ancestry.com provides, explore just one person at a time. From the home page, enter their full name using their surname, where they lived, and their birth year (or an estimate if you don't have the exact year). From there you can explore all that you can find for that one member. Narrow your search by adding life events and other family members. In the Support Center there are search tips which can be found by clicking on the Advanced Search at the top of the page. It helps if you know additional information about this member, such as their job, clubs they belonged to, their race, etc. You can search for exact matches or narrow your search by clicking Edit Search upon seeing the results.

From the Home page, you can select individual categories with the drop-down list under Search. If you do not see what you are looking for in the drop-down menu, select Search All Records and you can select a category or a subcategory from the list on the right side of the main search page. There are all sorts of options to select when searching by category.

4. View family trees of other people

Under Search, you can also find Public Member Trees. Searching other people's family trees can provide clues for your own family tree. From the Global Search, you can find Attached Records which often provide a wealth of information, including photos (whenever you see the camera icon), wills, and pages from family histories. You can tell how closely a person matches your search criteria, and how many other sources and/or attachments accompany the data. You will have better results by exploring the family trees that have sources, rather than those that are unsourced.

5. Connect with others, including possible relatives

When someone else is searching for your family, from the Owner icon you can click on to learn about the submitter of a family tree. How much you will be able to see will depend on the settings of the submitter. By clicking Contact, you can connect with the person if their settings allow for you to do so. When a person has saved the same record of a relative that you have also saved, there will be links to that record and to that person's family tree.

6. Search message boards and Scan online newspapers

Under Collaborate, you will find a link to Message Boards. Here you may find that someone else has already found the information that you are looking for. It's a good idea to check the places where your relatives may have lived, as well as their surnames. There are thousands upon thousands of boards and millions of posts available. Ancestry.com has a collection of historical newspapers. From Search All Records, scroll down Stories and Publication on the right, and you will find Newspapers. For free you will be able to search old newspapers. For a discounted price, subscribers can search a larger database in Newspapers.com. You can narrow your search by entering cities and/or states, and filter by entering dates.

7. Save your results

Save the records that you find on your family by printing all that is available (e.g., images, transcriptions, originals). Then put them together, and store in a dedicated space. You will also want to save records electronically by clicking the Save button in the upper right hand corner of the page. Here you can either attach the record to someone in your tree and store it in the Shoebox, and/or you may save it to your hard drive. The Shoebox items can be found at the bottom of the home page under Recent Additions. Once you have attached a record to your tree, you can use a free Ancestry.com app on your tablet or smartphone to view it later.

It's amazing how the discoveries made from tracing one's bloodline can produce substantial inner strength. The kind of strength that produces hope, grit, and perseverance. Ironically, the main source of this strength often comes from pain and suffering, and overcoming adverse circumstances. As Booker T. Washington put it, *"Let's keep before us the fact that, almost without exception, every race or nation that has ever got upon its feet has done so through struggle and trial and persecution; and that out of this very resistance to wrong, out of the struggle against odds, they have gained strength, self-confidence, and experience which they could not have gained in any other way."* Through this process, you should begin noticing many positive attributes that were passed down to you through your bloodline, and describe who you are today. Enjoy the journey!

Glossary of Terms

(Definitions are specific to how terms are used in this book.)

Attitude A way of thinking about someone or something, often reflected in positive or negative behavior.

Character Distinct qualities that make up one's personality and influence their behavior.

Cognitive behavioral theory Addresses how thoughts, beliefs and attitudes affect feelings and actions.

Constructive Positive, productive, and helpful manner of being, speaking, or offering advice.

Critical thinking Objective analysis based on facts, evidence, observation, and arguments prior to forming an opinion or judgement.

Delayed Gratification Resisting immediate pleasure to achieve a more meaningful experience later.

Ethnic Unity People of diverse ethnicities uniting respectfully and thoughtfully together around a shared purpose.

Evidence-based Effective approach based on practical application, research, and objectivity.

Groupthink Conforming to the ideas of the group rather than offering an individual thought, idea, or opinion.

Instant Gratification Giving in to the temptation of immediate pleasure at the expense of a more meaningful experience later.

Interpersonal relationships Any social connection between two or more people, i.e., family, friends, associates.

Law of suggestion A philosophy that explains how repetitive messages influence reality.

Leadership A practical skill that enables a person to guide and influence others toward the accomplishment of a goal, mission, or vision.

Legacy The impact a person's life makes on past, present, and future generations.

Mindfulness Meditations The state of being present and aware in the moment.

Mindset A mental attitude that determines how a person will interpret or respond to people, places, and situations.

Organized debate A contest of ideas formally discussed between two opposing sides, within a set of rules.

Personality theory Addresses how individuals think, feel, behave, and interact with their environment.

Rational emotive behavioral theory Addresses how thoughts and feelings positively or negatively impact behavior.

Self-awareness One's ability to understand their strengths and weaknesses and their ability to connect them to their thoughts, feelings, and actions.

Self-fulfilling prophecy A prediction or thought that becomes reality because of one's belief or expectation.

Solution-focused theory A goal-focused approach to positive change, where emphasis is placed on solutions over problems.

Strength-based theory A psychological approach that builds upon a person's existing strengths.

Success A self-identified measure of life fulfilment.

SWOR Analysis A framework used to evaluate barriers and solutions to desired personal and professional growth.

Wisdom The ability to think, act, and discern, based on experience, insight, understanding, common sense, and knowledge.

The End . . .
Is Only the Beginning

Made in the USA
Columbia, SC
31 March 2024

33854654R00091